SILENT VOICES

Rule by Policy on Canada's Indian Reserves

MEL BEVAN

Silent Voices

Tellwell Talent
www.tellwell.ca

ISBN
978-0-2288-6156-0 (Hardcover)
978-0-2288-6155-3 (Paperback)
978-0-2288-6157-7 (eBook)

Table of Contents

Foreword

The first treaty signed on "Turtle Island" (North America) was three hundred and nineteen years ago. The Albany Treaty was called "The Great Peace." In the twenty-first century, Indigenous peoples are still encumbered with non-peaceful policies and legislation in Canada.

This book gives insight into the past and current practices of the Department of Indian Affairs, and the bureaucracy that limits a First Nation council to be the real voice through their electorate. The band members of the First Nation are subject to numerous 'dos and don'ts' from the Indian Act in Canada's Constitution section 91(24). The interpretation of section 91(24) has long shadows through arbitrary practices by different department staff within Indian Affairs. In many instances, the voice, needs, and freedom of band members do not really filter to the top. The Minister of Indian Affairs has the ultimate power over elected band councils.

My forty years of experience as an administrator for First Nations operations both at band council and Indigenous organizations attests to the above fact. Quite often, I faced bureaucrats who believed that their minister had the "ultimate power" and ruined many good programs and promising ones too.

The author mentions that the majority of Canadian society of have many myths about Indians living on reserves. These myths create racism against Indigenous people in the long run. The real truth has not subsided racist attitudes today.

Reconciliation is the current societal topic. Real reconciliation will not happen until the Indigenous people's voices are heard and respect if given around their rights to their lands. Their lives can move forward and not be hindered by the Indian Act and the practices created from it.

What is needed from federal and provincial politicians is a political will for action so that changes can really happen. Indigenous voices need not be kept SILENT!

—Ray Jones

Acknowledgments

Longtime friend and advisor, Métis lawyer Mark L. Stevenson for reviewing the book, providing good suggestions, and correcting my legal inaccuracies.

Close friend and lawyer, Albert Peeling, one of the finest legal minds in Canada, for the countless hours of legal debate and philosophical discussion on the effect of law and policy on the lives of Canada's Indigenous people.

Good friend and confidant, Rod Link, retired editor of the Terrace Standard weekly for his excellent advice to put more of myself into the book.

My children and grandchildren for their unwavering support.

Author's Personal Note

I am forever grateful to those great past Native leaders to whom we as a people owe so much. These great leaders understood the importance of never losing our identity as a people of North America. I'm grateful not only for the lessons of the great well-known leaders, but more importantly the countless unsung heroes who stayed home to be the managers and workers. There are no books written about them, no achievement awards, no pat on the back . . .

This book is about the lessons I have learned over the past sixty years from these leaders, managers and workers who were my teachers and accomplices. It is their work in finding or inventing ways to do the impossible that has kept us together as a people.

I thank you, my friends.

CHAPTER 1:

The Only Home We Have

Suppression of a segment of the population continues to exist in Canada as public policy without purpose.

The quote made famous by Albert Einstein, "the definition of insanity is doing the same thing over and over again and expecting different results," cannot be more true than when defining and understanding the effect of the laws, policies and practices governing the lives of Indigenous people living on Canada's Indian reserves.

Justin Trudeau became Prime Minister in 2015 supported by First Nations (FN) across Canada because of a major promise to Canada's Native people to find solutions to the deplorable living conditions of the majority of people on Canada's reserves. The promise was seen by most First Nations (FN) people as hope for real and lasting change. Although it was an honest effort with no apparent lack of trying by the prime minister, the brief flash of hope not only failed but the frustration of failure has dampened the resolve of the Canadian Government to try again. The failure is viewed by FN organizations as a broken promise, but it can be more accurately described as an impossible promise. A promise made impossible by the crushing weight of history.

Long-standing British and Canadian public policy, supported by misinformed public opinion, negates any chance of real and lasting change on Canada's Indian reserves. The body of laws, policies, rules, and solutions used by Canadian and provincial governments since confederation, along with the acceptance of Canada's Native leaders, have created a system of management enveloping the people living on Canada's Indian reserves. Native leaders accept the laws, policies, and rules not because they generally agree with them, they accept them because they have little or no alternative.

The people who live on the reserves have no method of changing their living conditions. The Indian Act and its regulations, along with rules, policies, and political decisions both national and provincial, collectively fabricate and entrench a self-correcting and self-perpetuating system. The overall system fosters disfunction, and the disfunction created by the system fuels the system in a never-ending circle. Because the system is self-correcting, any improvements achieved by the progressive leaders of some communities, reverts to the original conditions or even becomes worse when progressive leaders are eventually replaced.

The federal and provincial governments and the First Nations leaders expend all of their time and energy attacking the symptoms and just as much time and effort avoiding the root causes of the problem created by Canada's laws, policies, and practices. History has no record of any political will from either the government of Canada or the FN leaders to tackle the root cause of this decline in the people's standard of living. Each have their own reasons.

Every national attempt at change has ended in failure for FN people: Royal Commissions, national inquiries, supreme court wins, studies, workshops, training programs, and mountains of dust-gathering recommendations have had little effect on the lives of FN people. The sum of all actions and policies of colonial governors, laws and policies created and enforced by successive governments of Canada, and the refusal of provincial and territorial governments to consider residents of Indian reserves in the same context as their respective citizens has deeply entrenched the deadlocked public policy of Canada. First Nations organizations, band leaders and their managers, consultants and lawyers must also bear the burden of failed initiatives; they all played a major part in maintaining and perpetuating the endless struggle to nowhere.

One group of people, the subject of this book, watch helplessly from the sidelines. The people living on Canada's Indian reserves. The question often asked is why do the people insist on staying on the reserves? Why don't they leave if living conditions are so far below the standard of those enjoyed by their fellow Canadians?

The reasons for staying are many. The reserves are all that is left of their ancestral homelands and is still the only home they have. It is the home where they feel welcome and safe. It is where they feel comfortable. A place where they are not considered different by their neighbours. A place where they can speak their own language and practice their culture without being looked down upon. Most importantly, it is the home of friends and family. They have no desire to abandon these homelands, even if all they have is hope. It is the one place they can enjoy themselves and experience freedom from discrimination. They are the group of people who are not council members, nor are they band employees; they have no basic human rights, and so they are the voices no one hears.

The reality of being Indigenous in Canada is the product of Canadian laws and public policy developed by the senior managers of the government of Canada and the provinces, better known as the bureaucrats who administer the laws and create the public and administrative policy. Prime ministers, Indian Affairs ministers and governments come and go, the real drivers of Indigenous policy in Canada are the employees of the federal and provincial governments of Canada.

Canada treats Indigenous people differently from all other Canadians not because of colour or race; it is the result of the long held European view of Indigenous peoples around the world. The European view of Indigenous peoples since the days of exploration can be described with their own words—primitive, uncivilized, innocent, lacking capacity and so on. It is tempting to attach the label of discrimination, but the label would simply belittle the complexity of the Canadian Indigenous condition. Canada could pass a law making it illegal to discriminate against Native people, but all everyone would have to do is to say they don't discriminate. Nothing would change, and discrimination would continue unabated. The law might even be another barrier for Native people because it would justify the official "equal but separate" policy championed by many of today's leaders.

An example of equal but separate is education on Indian reserves. Native leaders demand that the quality of education on reserves be equal to provincial standards, but at the same time reject the idea of provincial involvement in the operation of their schools. The provinces also argue the cost of building infrastructure needed for proper schools, high schools in particular, prohibits moving toward real equality. Provincial school boards also cite the high cost of upgrading schoolbooks, teaching materials and teachers' qualifications. It was the provinces' disinterest in providing education to Native communities that made possible the rise of residential schools and Indian day schools.

CHAPTER 2:

My Story

Placed in the shadow of the profusion of wealth by design

My story is the story of the Aboriginal people of Canada, the people who live on the Indian reserves of Canada. This is the real story. A story of the forgotten peoples of Canada, forgotten not only by the federal and provincial governments of Canada, but also more and more forgotten by their own leaders. I know this because I was one of those leaders and have been for the past fifty years. This book is based on my actual experience and the events and actions I have witnessed and worked on over the years as a council member, chief councillor, band manager, chief executive officer, regional leader, accountant, treaty negotiator, consultant, and financial advisor. I also have spent many years being involved in provincial and national Indian politics, along with all the perks and privileges that come with being part of the new elite.

I have spent a lifetime trying to understand the underlying reasons for the declining fortunes of the people living on the reservations and the rising fortunes of Native leadership in Canada.

I was born in 1941. It was a time when the Native people of Northern British Columbia were still able to use the land, and they had resources around them that allowed them to prosper and maintain much of their way of life. Before the beginning of World War II, the Native population in the north still outnumbered the non-Native population and were a major contributor to the economy of the region. The northern economy still relied on strong backs and local knowledge. The Native people excelled in gathering resources through commercial fishing, logging, and exploration. Trapping for a living was still practiced by many. Gathering of natural foods, hunting wild game, salmon still being abundant, along with good land to grow enough food was still possible in a largely unsettled north.

The war brought large numbers of new people to the north. Firstly, they came to build the infrastructure for defence against invasion and to be the defenders against an expected Japanese attack on the north coast. Secondly, there was the arrival of large numbers of Europeans displaced by a war-torn continent, and they were to build infrastructure and operate the new machinery of a wide-open north.

I have seen Native people's access to those lands and resources slowly vanish. The wealth provided by the lands and natural resources relied on by the original residents were slowly being replaced by substandard social services and ill-conceived programs delivered by successive band councils and band staff.

I have seen the decline of trapping for a living. Wildlife is now managed to accommodate the sport industry. The salmon runs are now a small percentage of what they were only fifty years ago. The land my grandfather and I once roamed freely on is now private property with *no trespassing* signs. The resources available to Native people in the north can no longer sustain anyone. The laws, including the ever-growing common law, along with practices and policies of the past allowing Native people to sustain themselves are still in place, but the lands and resources which allowed a degree of independence and self-reliance have all but disappeared.

My home community built their own school in the early 1900s to avoid sending their children to residential schools. In my home community, the school was ruled by the church, and the rule of the church extended into the everyday life of the people living in the community. I had the good fortune of being born to a mother whose wisdom kept our language and culture alive in our home; only our own language was spoken and was kept a secret from the church. In my youth, Native communities were neither governed by democracies nor a hereditary system; they were, in practice, theocracies.

My mother's advice was "do not believe anything they tell you without thinking it through carefully." I was lucky to have grown up at home. And because of my mother's wisdom and advice, I never had it beaten into me that I was inferior, nor did I ever allow myself to be convinced of that. I have lived my entire life equal to everyone else in Canada, despite the fact I have never been considered by my fellow Canadians as an equal, nor have I been treated as an equal.

Part of the ancient philosophy that my family teaches is that every problem has a root cause. Once you find the root cause, you will see that the solution is always in the root. What is the root cause of the endless struggle?

It was in the spring of 1957 when I had turned sixteen that I was first awakened to the real power of the Indian Agent. I began to realize just how helpless the people on reserves were to have any say in their own lives.

Before Christmas of 1956, I was told I had tuberculosis (TB) and sent to Miller Bay Indian Hospital near Prince Rupert BC. Miller Bay was an unused Canadian army hospital built for an expected Japanese invasion. No invasion ever came, but there was an epidemic of TB amongst Native people, and since provincial hospitals refused to accept Native people into their hospitals, Miller Bay Hospital was used as a TB hospital for Native people. In the spring of 1957, while I was in the hospital, a number of houses burned to the ground in my home community, and two of the houses belonged to my family.

My mother, who was chief councillor at the time, requested a release of the band's money earned on the reserve to rebuild the homes. The band funds were held in trust by the Department of Indian and Northern Affairs as required by the Indian Act. The request was refused. The reason was given in writing and signed by the Indian Agent: the band was diminishing in population and would soon be extinct, and so it was pointless to waste money. There is no appeal available for an Indian Agent's decision. The decision of the department to deny rebuilding our homes had a direct effect on me. I left the hospital Christmas of 1957, homeless with my only possessions on earth being a set of clothes my sister bought for me. I had outgrown everything I wore when I was admitted to the hospital.

Elected to the band council in 1962 at the age of twenty-one, I began a lifetime of learning and trying to understand why we are treated differently from the rest of the people of Canada. In the 1950s and 1960s, the common belief by the government of Canada was that Native people were well on their way to extinction. We were told by the Indian Agent that there was no point in making long-term plans or improvements in our community because in fifty years, there would be no Indians or Indian bands left in Canada. I learnt in 1962 that the policy of the government of Canada is to gradually remove the people from the reserves and eliminate all the reserves in Canada. The White Paper of 1969 was the government's attempt at legally implementing the long-standing policy.

The Indian Agent, under the Indian Act's definition of superintendent, is an extension of the minister. In the 60s, the Indian Agent was in charge of everything to do with our lives. Our only role on council was to do as we were told. Council meetings were called by the Indian Agent or the assistant agent. The agenda was prepared by the Indian Agent. There was very little discussion on any issue. The agent's job was to shape our thinking, through controlling information, to whatever end they had in mind for the reserve. The council meeting's agenda usually consisted of tasks that the department required to be done. Band Council Resolutions (BCRs) and any correspondence were prepared in advance. Our only role was to listen, sign and move on to the next item on the agenda.

The title of Indian Agent is no longer used in 2021 but continues to exist with the same unrestrained powers under different titles. The term "Indian Agent" was the official title used by the government of Canada for senior bureaucrats in department offices throughout Canada. A personal incident in 1949 illustrates the high regard Indian Agents had of themselves: I had won an award for something I wrote, and the Indian Agent heard about it. When he shook my hand, he told my mother, "He is going to be an Indian Agent some day."

I still remember our attempt at rebellion against the Indian Agent. The BC Department of Highways wanted some acreage for highway construction through one of our reserves and had offered us twenty-five dollars per acre. We said the going rate for the surrounding land was one hundred and fifty dollars per acre, and we would take no less. The Indian Agent told us he would take our demands to the province and get back to us. At the next council meeting, he showed us a letter signed by the British Columbia Minister of Highways with an ultimatum. We either agreed with the twenty-five dollars per acre, or the province would expropriate under Order in Council 1036 and we would get nothing.

So much for our rebellion.

Little has changed for the people on the reserves since my first term on council. Despite everything the Native leaders have tried over the years, the Department of Indian Affairs officials still retain the Indian Act power of yes or no. There is still no process or authority to appeal any action by the department. Nor is there any process or authority for the people to appeal any action by their own band council or band staff. Overly regulated programs are still created by the uninformed.

Paternalism is still official policy. The policy of communalism remains unchanged since colonial times. Unemployed Native people are still not counted by Statistics Canada, resulting in the ongoing exclusion of Native communities from regional development. A high unemployment rate on an Indian reserve is still considered a social problem and not an economic problem. The list goes on. The Canadian public still have the same negative view of Canada's Native people. The only constant is that the people's condition remains stagnant.

The one improvement is the opportunities leading to personal prosperity for the chief, the council members, and the band office staff. The opportunities, however, stop at the band office door in most cases, and the people living on Canadian Indian reserves can only look in with envy. The people are on the outside looking in and being left further and further behind by their own leaders and the government of Canada.

To write the truth about the Native experience, I recall reading and studying countless books, university studies, reports written by people using secondhand information or information gathered by authors from other works, and material gathered by writers through interviews or any other method. I write from my on the ground experience about the conclusions I have reached in a lifetime of reading, experiencing, listening to the people, and trying to make a difference.

One major discovered truth is no matter how hard we try, and no matter how hard we work to make the existing system function for the people living on the reserves, it is impossible to permanently change the lives of the people. In my travels across the country, I have seen communities with the good fortune to make changes and improvements in the quality of life for their people. The reason is always the same—the community is fortunate enough to elect a group of leaders with a caring staff. These leaders complement each other, and when working together, become greater than the whole. I have also seen some of the same communities experience a reversal of fortunes when electing a group with a sum of less than the whole. Once the progressive leaders are replaced, positive changes and improvements very quickly disappear.

The underlying question is: why are the people helpless to make changes, and why must they rely entirely on the character of their leaders to improve the quality of life on the reserves in a wealthy country like Canada? The simple answer is "that is how it is designed to work" and any progress is quickly reversed by the internal force of self-correction imbedded firmly into the system created by the Indian Act and the policies of successive governments since confederation. A system brought into existence by a bureaucracy simply doing their jobs. The bureaucracy cannot be blamed since they are merely carrying out the laws, policies, and instructions of their political masters.

CHAPTER 3:

Isolate and Assimilate

It is endless struggle for the right to live on our homelands and the right to keep our identity as Indigenous people.

The Indigenous people of Canada, referred to as "Indians" in the Canadian Constitution, are divided by circumstance into three groups. First, the people who do not live on the reservation. Second, the chief and council including the staff. The third are the subject of this book—the people who live on Canada's Indian reserves. The division into three groups is not a legal or a planned grouping, it is the result of the accumulation of federal and provincial laws, policies, and practices, both historic and current.

One of the groups are the Native people who do not live on Canada's Indian reserves. This group have by choice become part of the provincial framework. They are the people who choose to live in the cities, towns, and rural areas of Canada. Their story will require another book; even though they share the discrimination of their on-reserve relatives, their reality is vastly different. Each individual has their own reasons for living away from the reservation to which they are registered by the government of Canada. Native people have the same desire to exercise the basic human right of "free will" as anyone else in Canada.

The British and other European countries practicing colonialism have long denied Indigenous people basic human rights. After confederation, the government of Canada continued the practice. To this day, the denial of human rights is still practiced to a large degree. From its inception, the Indian Act put into law the practice of denying basic human rights to a single group of people. The suppression of "free will" is just one of those rights.

The Government of Canada—from the beginning—created and implemented two overarching public policies on Indian affairs to manage what was referred to as "the Indian problem." The first was isolation and the second was assimilation. Whether or not the government realized the two policies were in direct conflict with each other did not matter because the two policies were administered by two different groups of people. The irrational argument of keeping isolated Native people on reserves and at the same time expecting them to embrace assimilating into mainstream Canada was, and still is, a recipe for failure.

The Isolation Policy

The isolation policy of Canada was to remove Indigenous people and keep them separate from the general population. In the words of the policy: *"The dangers of complications with White men will thus be lessened."* To travel or move off the reserve required a permit signed by the Indian Agent. The requirement of a permit was not law, but the Indian Act endowed the Indian Agent with the power to make and enforce the policy. The policy, resisted by any means possible by the Native people, was scrapped in 1951. Indians were not legal persons which made it impossible for them to hold title to private land. The legal definition of a person of legal age in Canada was *any person except an Indian.* The only land they could use and occupy was on their home reserve.

Every registered Indian has a number. The first three numbers are the number of your home reserve. The old rule of *you must stay on your own reserve* exists to this day. To use and occupy any other reservation in Canada requires the approval of both the band council of the band you are leaving, and the band council of the reserve you wish to move to. Approval is not final until the minister's officials complete the process of changing your band number, and this rarely takes less than two years. The original public policy which created this absurdity no longer makes any sense to anyone, even to the department officials faithfully following the rules. No one knows why they are still doing it, but those are the rules. To change it requires the government of Canada to simply state it is no longer public policy and begin the process of dismantling the system.

Band numbers are long for a reason. The number is used by the government of Canada to provide instant information. The first three numbers are the number assigned to your home band. The last four numbers are your personal number. The remaining numbers were the religion you were assigned to (my religion code was UC for United Church), whether you lived on or off reserve, and whether you were male or female. The number is linked to a data base with all your information, birthdate, address, descendants, education, and any other information collected by the band over the years. In the age of reconciliation, all that is really needed is a simple ID card without a band number and without anything being linked to any data base.

Isolation of Native people living on reserves continues to this day. The isolation comes in the form of economic isolation and the deprivation of provincial services—services taken for granted by provincial citizens. The most noticeable isolated service is roads. Roads on or through reserves, although a part of and integrated into the provincial road network, are not built or maintained by the provinces. Grader operators and snowplow drivers are required by BC policy to lift their blades when passing through an Indian reserve. In British Columbia, road maintenance is privatized, and any equipment operator dropping his blade on a reservation out of the goodness of his/her heart can lose his/her job. I know this from personal experience when I asked an equipment operator if he could leave his brush cutter down on the road to my house, and he said, "I'd like to, but I will get fired if I do."

It is assumed by many, including Native people, that health care received by Native people on reserves is in addition to the health services provided by the provinces. Not so. Health services on reserves are instead of provincial services and are provided by the government of Canada not the province, unless they are paid in addition to health transfers by Canada. Provincial powers Clause 92 (7) of the Canadian Constitution reads: *"The establishment, maintenance, and management of hospitals, asylums, charities, and eleemosynary institutions in and for the province, other than marine hospitals."* No where does the constitution say, "except for Indians." In practice, however, it is "except for Indians."

I spent all of 1957 in an Indian TB hospital on the North Coast of BC. I have no complaint about the care provided by the dedicated and compassionate doctors, nurses, orderlies, and support staff. They were very respectful and provided the best care available to them. I owe my good fortune to write in 2021 to these good people. The downside is the reason Indian hospitals are necessary in the first place. Indian hospitals were necessary because provincial hospitals refused to admit Native people into their long-term care hospitals. Native people diagnosed with TB were simply sent home to die.

In 2021, Native children on Canada's Indian reserves are still excluded from the provincial school system. It may be believed by most people that this is just another conspiracy theorist myth, but it is a fact. Native children living in urban areas are a part of the general school population, but children on reserves are not. Each year, there is a head count of Native children attending public schools. The head count numbers are used by the Department of Indian Affairs to calculate annual monetary transfers to provincial school boards across the country. School boards operate with provincial funding which includes all of the students attending their schools. The millions transferred from the government of Canada are extra dollars for the school districts since their budgets are built on provincial taxes.

The Native people on reserves are not considered part of the economic fabric of Canada. When Statistics Canada calculates unemployment numbers in Canada, the federal policy is to officially exclude Native people, along with prison inmates and people with disabilities, from the numbers. In non-Native Canada, the unemployment number is an economic indicator to assist governments in monitoring the distribution of economic wealth. Unemployment is an economic problem, and Canada is obligated to take steps to stimulate economic activity. If an area of Canada has high unemployment numbers, the government of Canada and the provincial governments take action to create jobs.

Not so for Native people living on reserves.

By the policy of exclusion, an unemployed Native person is labeled a social problem, not an economic problem. The only action the government of Canada takes in areas of high unemployment with a high majority of Native people is to increase the budget for welfare payments. They make work programs to create temporary jobs for Native people, generally minimum wage jobs that are a far cry from subsidized industry. This is referred to by some as *corporate welfare*. The media will report there is a special fund set aside for Native communities, giving the impression the assistance is in addition to the funding available to all Canadians. Not so. Indian bands are not eligible by Canadian policy to apply for regional development assistance. They can only apply to those funds set aside for Indians.

Like most of Canada's Indigenous public policy, the economic exclusion policy goes so far back in time that it has become normal, and this has engrained the mistaken belief that it is as it should be. Ask anyone in government or any Native leader what the policy is for and prepare yourself for the deer in the headlights reaction.

Reconciliation is a meaningless exercise if these instruments of isolation remain in place. The list of policy instruments for isolation is a long one. Policy instruments were created by cabinet and can be rescinded one by one without fanfare by cabinet.

The Assimilation Policy

Once the isolation policy of keeping people on their home reservation was no longer enforced, the parallel policy of assimilation became the major policy initiative of the government of Canada. Assimilation was no longer in conflict with the policy of keeping the Native people separate and confined to the reservation. The method was to encourage the people to abandon the reserve by means fair or foul. The government could then declare vacant Indian reserves as surplus federal land and open these lands to developers. The legislation proposed by the 1969 White Paper was intended to do just that.

My home community is an example of the policy in action. In 1941, when I was born, the population was somewhere between 200 to 300. By 1960, the population living on my home reserve was zero. The band council I was elected to was like a government in exile since none of us lived on the reserve. There was no one left on the reserve. In 1964, I cleared a piece of land on a small reserve near Terrace, BC. Without permission, I built a home there. With my wife and son and the later addition of our daughter, we began the process of reclaiming our homelands with a population of four.

The final big push, by then Prime Minister Pierre Elliott Trudeau and Minister of Indian and Northern Affairs Jean Chrétien to finally implement in total the assimilation policy, came to a head with the 1969 White Paper on the elimination of reserves and status Indians in Canada. The actual effect of the proposed law was to unite Native people across Canada against the so-called White Paper, forcing the government of Canada to withdraw the proposal.

There is an often-asked question: if the reserves and the Indian Act are so bad, why fight to keep them? The real fight of the Native people of Canada is not to keep the reservation or the Indian Act. The Native people of Canada are fighting for their right to their homelands and the right to maintain their identity as Indigenous people. The objectives of the Indigenous people of Canada is largely misunderstood by our fellow Canadians. The misunderstanding by government officials is the most harmful.

Successive Canadian governments have conditioned the people of Canada to believe that the substandard living conditions endured by First Nations people on Indian reserves in Canada is not only normal, but is as it should be. First Nations people are in fact no different from other Canadians. They have the same dreams and ambitions; they work and study with as much vigor as any other Canadian. The people of Canada are convinced and believe the reason lies in the character of the Native people of Canada. Most Native people living on the reserves, having known no other way of life, also have come to believe the current Indian condition is normal and is as it should be. Canadians believe it must remain this way because they are Indians. The Native people believe it must be this way because they have been led to believe the current laws, policies and practices are what make them Indian.

The public believe that the Indian condition is normal. They also believe the government of Canada's management of the Indian people is not to blame for the continuing problem. This belief is at the root of the flawed assumption that the problem is not the system designed by the government of Canada, but the **character** of the Indigenous people of Canada.

The truth is that the management system and methods used by Indian Act bands were created by the Department of Indian Affairs' bureaucracy and based on two fundamentally flawed premises. The first flawed premise is that the system was designed mainly to serve the needs of the government of Canada and not to serve the needs of the people living on Canada's Indian reserves. The second flawed premise is the long-held belief that Native people are not as progressive as non-Natives and must be treated differently. Furthermore, the task of designing this different system was placed in the hands of people who were the least qualified to do the job.

As an example, in the 60s, a band financial accounting method was designed by bureaucrats with no accounting knowledge. The department insisted that this system must be used by all bands. In normal accounting for companies, organizations, municipalities and all governments, operating funds are kept in one bank account and the various projects, programs or cost centres are kept separate by the accounting method using one set of books. Because of the belief that a character flaw in Native people would prevent proper financial management using something the bureaucracy considered too complex, bands were required to keep funds for the various projects, programs and any other cost centres in separate bank accounts. With each bank account having its own set of books and reports. This resulted in all bands, regardless of size, being forced to attempt to manage twenty to thirty bank accounts with twenty to thirty sets of books. Any person with any knowledge of accounting is fully aware this is the most absurd accounting method ever devised, but that is what the bands in Canada were required to use if they wanted to take over managing their own funds. It took over twenty years of total chaos for the bands and their auditors to convince the department that they only needed one bank account and one set of books.

The absurd rational used to create the accounting requirement persists to this day in other government departments. Some bureaucrats in Health Canada still think "their" money should not be mixed with Indian Affairs' money and insist on separate bank accounts and books. Provinces still shudder at the thought of provincial money co-mingling with mismanaged federal money and still request separate bank accounts and separate books.

The Department of Indian Affairs still to this day requires keeping every program and project separate in the books. The increasingly complex band administrations and financial management requirements are seriously hampered by this insistence of separation. Bands today operate with hundreds of separate bank accounts. A bookkeeper trying to record a payment he/she was instructed to make must find which of the hundreds of accounts the payment should be charged to; it requires an unbelievable memory. If an account is not found, the options are to create a new account or make a guess. The result over time with creating new accounts and making best guesses is the creation of financial statements which make no sense and are useless as a tool for decision-making.

We must reach far back in history to find and examine the roots of Canadian misconceptions to understand why Native people are treated differently from other Canadians. More importantly, why do governments and Canadians, including Native leaders and managers, believe they MUST be treated differently from other peoples of Canada?

CHAPTER 4:

Devolution

Responsibility without authority to be responsible is irresponsible.

Since the enactment of the Indian Act in 1876 to the amendments made in the 1951 and well into the 60s, it was the Indian Agent, or more correctly, the government agent, who was in complete charge of everyone and everything to do with the Native population of Canada. In practice, "in charge" meant that council decisions required the Indian Agent's approval to be valid.

In the 60s, there was a move by the government to devolve or turn over some of the management of community tasks to the band councils. The first step was to create a band funding program called "band support funding" and create, by policy, a position of band manager. The actual powers of the band manager were, and are still limited to, having signing authority on such things a bank accounts, contracts, letters, etc., all subject to council approval. The Indian Agent could deal directly with the band manager without having to call a council meeting every time something had to be done. The band's management authority does not include any of the authority held by the minister or the minister's agents. There never was a transfer of authority to the band councils, only a devolution of responsibility. And because of the way it was developed, it was more imposed than devolved.

The devolution of First Nations band management was designed by the policy-makers of the Department of Indian Affairs—in isolation from the Native people. The intention was to off load but maintain control. The illogical premises or fallacies ingrained at the time are still ingrained to this day. The policy-makers then and now continue to be completely baffled as to why the systems they designed do not have the anticipated or planned results. The question guiding the policy-makers was: how do we allow them to do things for themselves and maintain our control at the same time? Maintaining control in practice means any and every change requires the approval of someone in the department chain.

Process of Approval

Every innovation proposed by people in the bands to make improvements requires departmental approval, and this continues to be an insurmountable obstacle in the attempt to make meaningful community progress. Any idea, good or bad, must go through the departmental approval process. Every innovation from communities must have district approval and then be recommended for regional approval. If an innovation is approved by the region, it must be reviewed by an unknown number of policy analysts before it is recommended to what is referred to as headquarters.

Headquarters then recommends the innovation to the treasury board. Treasury board has two main criteria. First, does the recommendation fit the policy objectives of the current government? Second, does it fit within the total budget parameters? After the national budget is passed in parliament, it becomes the task of the policy-makers to develop the guidelines and rules of the innovation, then back down the system. The entire process takes two years, and the resulting program generally has little resemblance to the original idea.

Progressive community leaders have learnt not to waste their time attempting to improve the system. They simply ignore the system by refusing to attend the endless stream of meetings designed to keep everyone in line. It is the government approval requirements and their requirement to be involved in all band decisions that spawns and fuels the meeting and travel industry so treasured by the Native leaders.

Fair Play and Democratic Rights

When it comes to First Nations people living on Canada's Indian reserves, principles of fair play and democratic rights that apply to Canadian citizens go out the window.

Property rights of the people of North America are denied to the Native people of Canada. The right to hold their leaders accountable is denied. Freedom of the press is denied to the people. Freedom of speech is denied. The right of all Canadians to be part of planning their future is denied. Mobility rights in the Charter of Rights and Freedoms guaranteed to Canadians are denied. For a band member to move from one reservation to another, the approval of the band council of both communities need to agree with final approval of the minister. My lawyer friends will claim vigorously that reserve residents have rights, and they are correct in theory, but in practice, the people have no rights.

Rights without government protection by law, nor protection by police, nor protection by Canadian courts are empty rights.

The general population of Canada find this difficult to believe. They believe equal rights in Canada applies to all, including Native people. One example of unequal rights is homeownership. Canadians, including Native people who do not live on Indian reserves, have the right to own their homes, including the land under their homes. This right is enabled and protected by numerous laws with two basic laws providing the property right foundation. Clause 94 (13) of the Canadian Constitution gives the provinces the exclusive authority over "property and civil rights in the province." Each province has a Land Title Act which lays out by law how land ownership is recorded, registered, and protected. The provinces of Canada have a duty to protect the registered private property of their citizens. This duty includes the entire legal system, including the police and the courts. The government of Canada also has laws protecting and promoting private ownership such as the National Housing Act and the Canada Mortgage and Housing Corporation Act (CMHC). Property rights for Canadians is an individual right. Native people living of Canada's Indian reserves have no such protection nor any equivalent protection.

Indian reserves are federal land. The Indian Act defines a band as: *a body of Indians for whose use and benefit in common, lands, the legal title to which is vested in Her Majesty, have been set apart before, or after September 4, 1951.*

Legal title is vested in Her Majesty is the key phrase in the definition. Indian reserves are the property of the Crown, and it is this property right of the Crown which is protected by the provincial legal systems. The property right belongs to Her Majesty and not to the people living on the reserve. Native people's property rights on a reserve are limited to living on it, not owning the lot with their home. The right to use and benefit is a communal right, not an individual right. On reserves, CMHC's role is to protect the rights of the Crown and the banks.

The Canadian Constitution does not say Native people's rights are to be excluded, but because of section 91(24), government policy-makers have interpreted the clause to mean Native people living on reserves are noncitizens and are therefore not entitled to the same rights as other Canadians.

Denial of rights has its roots in the Indian act, in common law from cases on the Indian Act, and government Indian public policy. Canada's Indian public policy of viewing Native people as different and inferior to Europeans began long before confederation and continues to this day. The history of the suppression of Indians in Canada is long and well-studied and recorded by numerous writers.

This public policy is continued and is compounding with every attempt by successive Canadian and provincial governments using information and methods of preceding governments.

CHAPTER 5:

Hiring Your Own Master

Democracy is an Illusion when the people governed have no voice.

Even though the people on reserves elect their own chief and councils, they are in fact ruled and not led by the people they elect, and the elected people are driven by masters beyond their control.

In the 1950s and 1960s, the elected leaders were with the people below the line that separated the FN people from the government of Canada. The leadership at the time worked diligently for the people who elected them. These were the leaders who led the fight against the 1969 White Paper, designed to eliminate the Indian identity in Canada. The battle was won by those great leaders of 1969, and a new way of interacting with Canada began. The recognition of Indian leaders, and the realization by governments across the country that they must deal with the so-called Indian problem, gradually changed the role of Indian leaders on reserves.

At first, the Native leadership held the upper hand in the new relationship mainly because governments and the bureaucracy did not have the means nor the know how to handle this new power. With unlimited resources available to the various government departments, such as the Department of Indian and Northern Affairs and the Department of Justice, to put to work consultants, public relations professionals and many other experts to design ways to control the problem while at the same time appearing to be cooperative, the balance of power gradually evaporated. The current leaders carry with them the illusion of power and the people back on the reserves are made to believe they have democratic power. That democratic power is of course an illusion.

A basic principle of democracy enclosed in the quote by Abraham Lincoln "government of the people, by the people, for the people" is missing on the reservation. Only the first applies—they get to elect the chief and council. As for the second principle, the people are governed by the Minister of Indian and Northern affairs via the Indian Act and not by the people they voted for. The third principle is nonexistent because the chief and council do not have the power to govern anyone without the permission of the minister. The democratic principle of representative government has never been part of the reservation system. The chief and council might have began attempting to be representative governments, but with no power to actually make any changes, they have evolved to representing themselves. The communal fallacy requires the governments to consider the chief and council not as representatives of the people but as the only entity they will interact with.

Democracy which excludes certain groups of people is not uncommon in the Western world. One of the most democratic countries in the world, the United States of America, excluded Indigenous Americans and Black people from being part of the democracy. In the USA, all men are created equal did not mean all men were equal. South African apartheid is well-known. Australia's Aborigines are treated the same as Canadian Indigenous people.

All of these and many other democracies owe their origins to Great Britain. The same policies and beliefs of supremacy used to govern British colonies are still being followed diligently by successive governments of Canada. The belief is so prevalent that it is considered by the majority of the Canadian population to be the norm, and keeping Native people where the majority believe they should be is the accepted condition. The reason of course is "because they are Indians."

Since confederation, and eleven years after the passing of the first Indian Act, the minister has been the governor of all Indians and lands reserved for Indians. The Indian Act passed after confederation bestowed upon the minister the designation of *Superintendent General of Indian Affairs.* The Indian Act is a creature of section 91(24) of the then British North America Act, which in 1982 became the Canadian Constitution, and section 91(24) of the constitution separates Indians from the rest of Canadians. The only reason the provinces do not provide public services to FN on reserves is a lack of compassion and political will. Nothing in the constitution requires provinces to refuse services.

Today in 2021, the minister still rules. In practice, it is the employees of the department under the minister who are the real rulers. In the 1950s, they were called Indian Agents and had the last word on every part of Indian life. It was said that the Indian Agent controlled everyone from the cradle to the grave. The statement was true then and is still true today. Although, today the power is exercised in a carefully planned way to appear kinder, gentler, and more politically correct, but in the end, the last word still belongs to the minister and his/her employees. In the 1950s, when the Indian Agent meant "no" he said "no." Today, under the new title of Finance Officer, the Indian Agent says, "You can do whatever you like, but we will not be able to continue funding you." The department has always punished uncooperative leaders by punishing the entire community. Why? Because they are deemed communal.

For the people being governed, the new Indian Agent is not only the department and its employees but includes the chief and council and band staff. The devolution that began in the 60s did not devolve authority, it only devolved management. The control of Indians from the cradle to the grave is now carried out by the councils and the staff using Department of Indian Affairs' policies and programs. The councils and band staff of today have many masters; the people are only masters for one day every two years. For the next two years until the next election, the councils and staff serve other masters.

The Masters

In a democracy, the people are the masters that their governments must serve. On a reservation, this is not the case. Much of the band's resources are used to satisfy the demands of other masters.

The people are at the very bottom of the masters' list. They are the people who get to say, "Please, sir, can I have some more?" Democracy in North America was described as "government of the people, by the people, for the people." On Canada's Indian reserves, it is more accurately described as "government of the people, by the band staff, for the band council."

Indian and Northern Affairs Canada

In the United States, the Department of the Interior Bureau of Indian Affairs has evolved to be an advocate, working with the Native Americans with the goal of providing the same services to Native tribes that are similar to the services provided to other Americans. Though far from perfect, the Bureau of Indian Affairs describes on their website their "role now is as a partner with tribes to help them achieve their goal for self-determination while also maintaining its responsibilities under the Federal-Tribal trust and government-to-government relationship."

In Canada, there is no partnership between the Department of Indian and Northern Affairs and the FN people. Department officials claim they are working in partnership with Canada's FN people, but in fact that is not the truth. It would be more truthful to say the officials are attempting to work in partnership with the chief councillor.

To the Department of Indian and Northern Affairs, the FN people who are not on council are just numbers on a paper and not real people. To save money, for example, the department created the classification of on-reserve and off-reserve. Only on-reserve members who are members of that band are counted for funding purposes. Members of other Canadian bands who live in Native communities for family or other reasons are not counted; they are considered off-reserve because they are not living on their home reserve.

The councils and staff have been conditioned to enforce this without knowing the purpose is to keep the per capita numbers down. The band "members only" rule is another cost-saving device used by the department. Native communities across Canada, like other communities, are made up of various people. Like all other human beings, Native people move around. Bands across Canada are no longer populated by their own band members as was required one hundred years ago. The old rule of requiring the Indian Agent's permission to leave your reservation has changed to *you will only be entitled to services if you live on your own reserve.*

The only input bands have in the budgeting process is to count heads. Head count of band members living on reserve, members of other bands and non-Native spouses and relatives are not counted, numbers of band members on social assistance and numbers of band members in elementary school. These numbers are the only contribution bands have in the annual budgeting process. Each year, near the end of March, the band receives a budget document from the department for them to sign and return before the end of March. Any attempt to negotiate better numbers means no funds in April—the "punish them all" principle. Partnership in words only, master in practice.

The needs of the department are the priority of the department employees. Through control of finances, the band councils serve the needs of the department. There have been so many lawsuits won against the department since the 1950s that the department conducts all of its business with FN with the mandate of protecting the government of Canada as their primary job.

Writing reports on every program is a department policy requirement. The purpose of the reports is to fulfill the departments policy of using reports as a tool for accountability. There are far too many reports generated annually, so no one has time to read them all, but the department can report to parliament and the Canadian public that the accountability requirement has been fulfilled. All written and financial reports go to the department and not to the people. Writing and processing these reports costs millions of dollars every year and is a major part of the consultant industry. Every initiative, major or minor, has a report writing section of the budget to cover the cost of writing a report. The reports are usually written by professionals who are familiar with the format preferred by department officials.

For the department to continue blaming the FN for creating their own problems, the department needs to continuously look good and be seen to be making every effort to make improvements. To be clear: the department's need to look good is not for the benefit of FN people, it is for the benefit of the Canadian public because it is the public that drives the department. The majority of Canadians believe all the FN's problems, such as housing, education, unemployment and everything else is of their own creation. The majority believe that helping only make it worse. The department makes no effort to correct that misconception.

One of the tools used by the department to look good is the "Favourite Community" tool. Communities who go out of their way to follow all of the rules, make the right speeches, and please the right people, tend to have far more department funding and more paid travel to major centres than other bands. Generally, bands with good press and good photo ops receive far more attention and more dollars for administration. It is never revealed that except for a chosen few, the lives of the people not only remain the same, but in some cases, get worse.

One of the most needlessly costly endeavors of the department is building of community infrastructure, such as water systems, roads, and construction of subdivisions. Bands have no legal authority to borrow money in the same way municipalities can to build community infrastructure. Municipalities can spread the cost of major projects over long periods whereas bands must pay it all in one year.

One consequence of this legal difference is costly temporary solutions can go on for years. Millions of dollars are spent each year, for example, in hauling water at the cost of $30,000 to $50,000 per month into communities with problematic water systems. The bands have no control of the design or construction methods in building infrastructure. Designs are done by department approved consultants who pay no attention to local knowledge or local conditions or even local needs. The guidelines developed behind closed doors must be followed at all costs. The councils and staff have no problem with temporary solutions because it takes the problem off their hands and means more dollars to spend.

The department's management of community infrastructure is ludicrous to community members who can only stand back and watch. They cannot say anything because it is believed by all to be a communal problem; individuals have no voice.

The Auditors

One of the masters the bands must cater to is the auditing firm they hire to audit their finances. It may sound ridiculous to be required to hire your own master, but on Canada's Indian reserves, ridiculous is the norm. The auditing instructions do not come from the band, the instructions come from the Department of Indian Affairs.

Most band accounting systems are designed to satisfy the needs of the auditor if they are to properly follow the department's instruction. Auditors prefer the simplest type of bookkeeping which only records cash received and cash spent. The cash system is the easiest to audit but the most useless for management purposes.

Band Office Staff

Regardless of how dedicated some staff members are in trying to help band members, the fact is they are no different from anyone else in the work force—it is still their own paycheque that matters. The primary concern of employees everywhere is to keep their job.

Making the chief and council members look good and satisfying the needs of external funders comes ahead of keeping band members happy. Speaking out for band members is fatal, jobwise, for band staff. Because there are no rules or standards for staff to follow, they can basically devise their own job descriptions. If there are rules, such as a human resource policy, it is the staff who write them or instruct the consultants hired to write the policy. The result is that policy and guidelines favour the staff over the band members. Even though the staff report to the councils, it is the staff who make recommendations to the councils.

Band offices are set up to manage the band office and the needs of the chief and council and not the needs of the people. The only time the needs of the people are considered is when there is program funding available and a proposal must be put together. Because programs are developed in some unknown room somewhere near Lake Ontario, the program criteria generally have no resemblance to the communities' actual needs. The management rule is to *make the proposal fit the criteria, and if no problem exists, make one up.*

Consultants

Native communities across Canada are awash with consultants. They are not only working for the bands but for governments and industry too. All are self-identified experts on FN affairs. All it takes to be a Native expert is to work in government or industry on some Native files, add it to the resume, and through some magic become an expert. The use of consultants is another example of hiring your own master.

Consulting on FN issues is a lucrative industry. Although there are many who do excellent work and produce good results, there is no way for bands to determine if the advice is the right advice for their circumstances. The progress of a FN community is equal to the talents of the consultants they hire.

Consultants only know what they know and will channel the leadership into the direction of their knowledge area. Consultants do not arrive at the door with the intent of learning about the people; they only arrive with their own knowledge which was acquired elsewhere. The usual result is that the need for the consulting firm to add to their resume becomes paramount to the needs of the people in the community. Unintentionally, this becomes another situation of a master bending and directing the leadership.

The best-known consultants who do the best work are those who stay with one community for years, understand the people, become part of the local culture, study local economic conditions and develop a real kinship with the people in the community. They are the consultants who know, like all towns and cities of Canada, Native communities are not all the same.

Indian Organizations

Band councils are not legal entities under the laws of Canada and do not have the legal authority to form organizations. Bands over the years have had to dream up inventive methods to accomplish objectives that are beyond their powers. Because band council lack the authority to form regional and provincial organizations, it has become the standard practice to create organizational entities using the provincial non-profit Societies Acts. Since the council is not a legal entity, the founders of Indian organizations must be individuals as required by provincial law. Indian organizations are, in legal fact, groups of individuals not groups of FN bands. If an organization stays on track and limits itself to the purposed goals it was set up for, an organization can be effective.

Most Indian organizations start in response to a collective problem or at the request of the government of Canada or the provinces. The chart of organizations all starts with the people across the top with the chief and councils below the people, followed by the executive of the organization and staff. Using the Societies Act is the ultimate 'fit the square peg into a round hole' problem.

First is the problem of membership. In a non-profit society, it is the members who are in control of its operation. They are required by law to approve such things as audit reports. With an organizational chart showing the people at the top, it is reasonable to believe the members should be the people. However, for logistical and cost reasons, it is not only impractical but impossible for the people to be members because it could never be possible for the members to meet.

So, the people are gone.

The next line on the chart is the chief and council, but since they are not a legal entity and have no authority to form organizations, they cannot be members as chief and council—they can only be members as individuals. Since they were elected to represent the people, once they act as individuals, they separate themselves from the people who elected them.

So, the elected representatives are gone.

The executive is in turn elected or appointed by individuals, and they end up as the only ones at the top of the chart. Reporting to the people becomes a matter of policy rather than a legal requirement.

The second problem is the purpose of organizations. The purpose of an organization depends on the reason for starting it. Although organizations in general have a very low success rate, they are essential because no effort has been made to try to find a better way to address collective problems. All organizations basically have the same structure required by the Societies Act. Some are established to tackle a single problem and can be referred to as single purpose organizations.

Single purpose organizations work well at first while everyone agrees unity is the best way to proceed. Unity by its nature is extremely short-lived; it exists only while people are all in one room and have a sense of being of one mind. The only real unanimity is the agreement that there is unity. It fades very quickly once the participants return to their respective communities. Once they are back to the real world of everyday duties dealing with local issues, the department and the numerous other organizations and boards, group priorities are very quickly sidelined for real world priorities. There is always a small group of dedicated individuals who actually believe there is unity, and these are the people who actually take the time to tackle the common purpose. Without these dedicated individuals, organizations stand no chance of accomplishing anything other than organizing meetings and hiring consultants.

When a single purpose organization either completes the single purpose or everyone realizes nothing can be achieved, they need to decide what to do next. Organizations are seldom wound down as required by the Societies Act, but when no one can come up with another task requiring unity, they are simply abandoned and left to die or acquire a life of their own.

Once formed, organizations eventually take on a life of their own. It becomes independent of its founders. If there is good, dedicated leadership, this in itself is not a bad thing. It is only when the self-interest of the people involved play a greater role, and the organization is used for purposes never intended by the founders, that they no longer have a purpose. The Societies Act constitution usually has a long list of members, but there is no real requirement for members to meet. An annual general meeting report for the Register of Companies can be drafted by a lawyer and signed by the executive to stay legal. The membership list can be used as proof of its existence, even though the members no longer support or attend any of the meetings.

The real reason societies perpetuate themselves after the original task is complete is because executive has no instructions to shut it down and the staff and consultants need steady employment. Some single purpose organizations that perpetuate themselves become greater and accomplish greater things than what was originally envisioned by the founders. The growth of any organization depends entirely on the strength of the personalities of the leaders.

The solution to the management problems in Native communities can never be found in external organizations no matter how well they function because groups always place themselves above the communities and become another master.

The only organizations which function well are those created by either provincial or federal legislation. These are single purpose organizations, for example, land management or taxation. These organizations function well because they are established by law and federal regulation and not intended to be operated by political boards.

Power of the People?

Political power on a reserve has a different meaning than what it means in the rest of Canada. One meaning of power means having the legal authority to make things happen. On a reservation, neither the chief and council nor the people have any real legal authority—all the legal authority is held by the government of Canada.

The people have the legal authority to vote for their leaders every two years and that is pretty much the extent of their real power. Even if councils have general meetings, it is the staff and council who determine what information is put in front of the people. There is no legal requirement for the councils to follow the wishes of the people.

People have tried protests, sit-ins, complaining to the department, demanding proper reports, lawsuits, and all manners of effort to find a way to increase their power. Any success the people have in increasing their power over the council is short-lived. Because councils are not actually required to do anything, they simply ride it out. They can agree with the people, saying they will do what the people want and then do nothing. Since the Department of Indian Affairs' only connection with the band is with the band council, the people are usually simply labeled by the department as disgruntled, and they consider the episode a local issue for the council to handle.

In a constitutional democracy, the power to govern is derived from the people. Under the Indian Act, the powers of the chief and council are derived from the minister and cabinet.

It is the councils that hold all the power—real or perceived power—in any Native community, and it is the chief councillor who has control over the council. There is a belief among the band members that the extent of the chief's power is to chair and break ties in council meetings. The tie-breaker argument has been used at every dispute between the people and the band councils. The argument has never worked, but people still hang on to it as a thread of hope. The reality is that council members are only councillors when the majority act together, and the chief councillor as an individual is chief councillor 24/7 for the full two years.

Extraordinarily little can be said about the power of the people on the reserves because they have so little power. At national and provincial conferences, the little people stand and give passionate speeches to applause and group hugs, and the exact same thing happens at band community meetings and in council meetings. The nature of band management in Canada is not set up to solve the problems of the people, even though that was the original intent. They have evolved to manage the activities of the chief and council, and the Department of Indian affairs.

There is a never-ending stream of people empowerment programs and service industries that has grown up around solving the people's powerlessness. All these empowerment projects begin from the assumption that it is a flaw in the people's character that needs fixing. No amount of people empowerment training can change the power structure on Canada's reserves; only the Parliament of Canada can do that.

While the intent of empowerment initiatives may be well-intentioned, the development of these empowerment programs are in fact being developed by the same 'behind the doors developers' who perpetuate the imbalance of power to begin with. The gap between reality and the flawed world of Indian reserves becomes even wider once consultants become involved in the delivery of programs such as healing, self-esteem building and all the other well-meaning initiatives. Because no amount of empowerment will make any difference to the way the system works, false hope is created and eventually turns into a sink hole of disappointment. The basic principle of most empowerment projects is *we know you are helpless, and we know it is not your fault, but we can help you feel good about it.* It is a never-ending cycle of ignoring the systemic nature of the people's powerlessness and pouring resources into improving the character of the people—in effect, blaming the people for their own powerlessness.

Democracy without untouchable rules can very quickly become dysfunctional. A true democracy works for the people. If there is an untouchable rule, that power is derived from the people. A perception of democracy, or more accurately, the illusion of democracy has no rule other than what is believed by the people being ruled. In Canada, there are no rules other than the Indian Act and the whim of the minster and cabinet, resulting in a wide range from democratically run communities to quasi dictatorships. All these communities are not stable because chief councillors operate without rules, create their own controls and can turn a democratically run community into a dictatorship or a dictatorship into a democratic community.

Such is the power of the people.

CHAPTER 6:

Introduction to Band Council

The desire to lead is basic human nature, the only difference is the objective.

The Indian Act requires the existence of a band council. The process for band elections was designed to make sure there is a band council whether the people wanted one or not. A band council is required because the government of Canada cannot interact directly with the Native people of Canada; they will only interact with a band council. The minister has the ultimate power over band councils. If the people refuse to conduct an election, the department will conduct one for them, and if no one shows up for the nomination or vote, the minister will appoint a council.

The nomination procedures under the Indian Act is unlike any process anywhere democracy is practiced. One of the most difficult problems of the operation of democracy is picking the individuals who are to run for office. Political parties all have various methods: municipalities use methods spelled out in provincial law, non-profit societies and groups attempt to find willing and able candidates to run for office. Whatever the method used, all the methods require the willingness and consent of the individual before they can be nominated. Candidates are required to play an active part in their own nomination. Not so under the Indian Act.

The huge numbers of people running in most band elections gives the public the mistaken belief that huge numbers of people want to be on council. Having ten to twenty people running for chief councillor and thirty to forty people running for council gives the Canadian public the impression that there is a real desire by large numbers of Native people to be involved in the political running of the band. Why are so many people running? The true answer lies in the Indian Act regulations on the nomination procedure.

The original intent of the Indian Act nomination procedures was to make certain there were candidates in the running whether or not they were willing or able. Candidates in band council elections did not even need to know they were candidates. The law has recently been changed to require the nominated to agree to leave their name standing, but there is still no requirement to agree to be nominated. There is no requirement for the nominated to show any indication of a desire to run. Any logical thinking person would find this to be an absurd way to run a democratic election, and they would be right if the intent were to run a democratic election.

To understand the problem requires a detailed examination of what happens during a nomination process.

The Band Council Nomination Process

The process begins with a date being set for a nomination meeting and a INAC approved electoral officer appointed. Historically, the electoral officer was the Indian Agent. Today, an independent electoral officer is appointed by the band council and must be approved by the department.

In democratic elections, the process of finding and nominating candidates is lengthy and can be complicated. The United States' presidential nomination process is close to two years long. In Canada, nominating party leaders can take years or however long the party executive decides. MPs and MLAs endure a lengthy elimination process. Municipal councils, school boards, reginal districts and all others have the nomination process open for more than thirty days. In all cases, candidates are generally required to file their own nomination papers, including signatures of support. No system is perfect, but the candidates should at least take steps to indicate a desire to be a candidate.

For Indian Act bands, the nomination process under the laws of Canada is two hours long, and there is no requirement for the candidate to indicate a desire to be on council.

The two hours begins with the announcement by the electoral officer, "The nominations are now open."

The nominations for the chief councillor and band councillors happens at the same time. The electoral officer is required to continuously repeat the phrase "Are there any further nominations?" for the full two hours. The constant repeating gives the people in the meeting the impression that they must find other people to nominate.

There are actual cases where people in a nomination meeting are flipping through the band list, trying to find more people to nominate. A motion to close nominations is not allowed—the clock must be run out. Because consent to be nominated is not required, this constant call for nominations results in huge numbers of people nominated who never had any intention of running for council. Recent amendments to the regulations still do not require consent to be nominated—only consent to remain on the nomination list.

In democratic nominations, the objective is to find the most qualified people or people who can demonstrate wide support. No so in band nominations. The objective is to get names on the ballot. A surprising number of people get nominated because they happen to be in the room or because someone in the room happened to remember them.

For the purposes of this examination, we will start with the chief councillor. Any person on the band list can nominate someone by saying in the meeting, "I nominate *so and so* for chief councillor." All that is required to nominate a chief councillor is for another person on the band list to say, "I second that nomination." If the person is in the room, he or she will be asked by the electoral officer if he or she agrees to remain on the list. If the person is not present, a letter will be sent to the person requesting their consent. And that is it, the person is officially nominated.

Before the law was changed, the person nominated was not required to consent to be on the ballot. And for chief councillor, there has never been a requirement for that person to be an

Indian on the band list. There is a process for withdrawing from running, but no process for agreeing to run. There is a set number of days in which a person can withdraw. If that deadline is missed, you are running for chief whether you like it or not. There was in recent times a requirement that the withdrawal notice had to be in writing and notarized by a notary public. This rule has been relaxed since even the department has trouble swallowing its own absurdity.

The absurd rules have resulted in some strange twists over the years. For example, the 'no response means consent' rule has resulted in individuals ending up on council without even being aware they were running. The rule that any Canadian can run for chief councillor of any band in Canada has resulted in some strange nominations. Regardless of who wins the chief councillor position, little change happens in the community, so elections are more like popularity contests rather than serious leadership selection. There are, of course, exceptions.

For the band councillor, the individual must be a band member on the band list. To be a resident in the community is not a requirement. In most cases, people who move to cities and elsewhere have no interest in what happens in their home communities, in the same way all other Canadians who move elsewhere in the world have little concern of the day-to-day activity in their hometowns. It is a perfectly normal human reaction. All people are more concerned with the action of where they are rather than where they were. It is the principle of wherever you go, there you are. In most cases, the band members living elsewhere are the majority.

In a two-hour nomination meeting, the people who actually want to stand for either chief or council are generally nominated in the first fifteen minutes. There are generally two groups. The first group are those who have their movers and seconders lined up and ready to go, the other group have no organization and use the hints to friends and crossed-finger method, hoping to be nominated. There are various reasons why people want to run for band council aside from the "because I was nominated" reason. There are those who have a real belief that they can make a difference. There are several main categories of people with a desire to make a difference.

The Movers

First are the movers and doers—the people who make things happen. These are the people who can usually succeed in making some improvement. They are the people who come with new ideas, and they not only know how to get things done but have the skills and drive to get rid of the old and build something better. The built-in limitations of band councils soon make improvement up to a point all but impossible. The law of diminishing returns kicks in very quickly on Canada's reserves. At first, change can come with ease and is extremely satisfying for the people when they see they have elected agents of change. The ceiling of progress established intentionally or unintentionally in Canada's Native communities is far below that of the rest of Canada. The effort required to get anything done increases daily, and it does not take long before the downward force of the Canadian reservation regime discourages even the most well-intentioned council members. Discouraged movers and doers generally mean the community returns to its original state.

It must be emphasized that failure to make permanent improvement may be common, but it is equally common for the movers and doers to succeed. Groups that succeed are those who have a clear understanding of how the system works. They understand the roadblocks. They know and acknowledge the limits and then find the allies within the system to create ways to overcome or bypass the limits.

Government bureaucracy has recognized the power and benefits of working with allies for progress and has attempted to institutionalize it through what they call *the partnership program*. Like all good ideas in the system, the partnership program has never worked. Anytime the department's bureaucracy attempts to implement an idea that requires working outside the system, they use the same tried and failed bureaucrats and consultants using the same tried and failed methods.

The Stoppers

Second are the people who are unhappy with what the current council and administration are doing. They run for council to do something about what they believe to be wrong. They are known as the stoppers—they stop everything. Unlike the movers and doers, the stoppers have no plan beyond the stopping action.

Like parliamentary opposition parties, they are particularly good at telling the leaders what they are doing wrong and demanding that they stop. The stoppers give the community members the notion that they will make the changes to the things they complain about. Once elected, the true stopper will continue to complain throughout their entire term in office. They will still demand change without realizing they are complaining about their own performance.

There is no doubt there are things happening in all communities that should be stopped, and sometimes the stoppers are what the community needs. The problem is the stoppers do not know when to stop stopping. If there are enough elected, then the community will practically grind to a halt. Band management in this case will shift into coast to wait it out.

Some of the staff are quite happy because their job description is reduced to getting to work on time, and if they do as little as possible, they will not be noticed. If they do nothing, there is nothing to stop. Some of the staff who are hardworking and have spent years making a real effort to accomplish something for the people quickly get discouraged and don't last long in these circumstances. There are many cases where this has happened and very few communities recover.

The movers and doers in the community no longer have the desire to be involved. Capable people avoid applying for work, and capable employees who leave have no desire to return. It must be restated at this point that the reason this happens is not the result of any character flaw in Native people but because of the absence of any rules and controls in the system similar to the rules and controls in non-Native communities across North America.

The Reasonable Voices

Third are the candidates who are neither movers nor stoppers and have a real desire to supply the voice of reason. There is always a conflict between the requirements of INAC, Health Canada, industry etc. and the real needs of the people living on the reserves. Council members benefit from catering to outside requirements, and that is a much stronger pull than the unrewarding task of community concerns. Without reasonable voices on council, the pull from the approval of external masters and personal gain eventually leads to the neglect of the people.

In most band councils across Canada, reasonable voices are the norm. These are the pragmatists on councils who put the people first and make a real attempt to maintain a balance between external pressures and the people. They are generally aware of the limits of council powers and make real efforts to direct diminishing resources to community well-being.

Most Native communities in Canada have reasonable voices on council and maintain stable administrations. These are the communities that no one hears about. They are never in the news, and the people—even with the absence of progress—live reasonably comfortable and content lives.

The voice of reason on Canada's reserves is diminishing in direct proportion to the rate that resources available to Native people are diminishing. Reasonable people feel the increasing pressure of diminishing resources, such as lack of housing, substandard education, and lack of basic services (i.e. clean water, decent roads). The most troublesome is the growing spread between the capped social services and the rising cost of living. This causes reasonable people to become more active beyond the reserve.

The power of the voice of reason diminishes exponentially beyond the boundaries of the reservation. Provincial and federal organizations may have been brought into existence to tackle problems in a reasonable way, but forces of self-preservation and the desire for personal recognition generally wrestle the voice of reason quickly to the ground. Even those in government who are sympathetic to the point of tears will do nothing more than bring out the tissue box.

The Returnees

A fourth group are the non-residents who set out to take control of a community. Takeover is not the correct term in this case because they are all band members who have chosen to exercise their right to vote. In most cases, they have legitimate concerns and have every intention to help to improve the lives of their families at home. With very few exceptions, there is no evil intent involved. The problem is most of the people have never lived or worked on a reservation and have as many misconceptions about Indians as everyone else in Canada. They have learnt that the problems are self-inflicted from their studies at university, the media, and an endless stream of complaints about Indians on reserves. And like all Canadians, they believe in the character flaw fallacy.

Many believe that all they have to do is use their knowledge and education about the people on reserves and all will be well.

Many do not last long and leave without really understanding the true cause of the obstacles faced by people living on Canada's Indian reserves. It should never be assumed that I am suggesting that educated and concerned people should stay away. The reservation may be an agonizing place to live to some one not used to it, but it is home, and for the Native people of Canada, the reservation is the last corner, however small, left of their original homelands. The people living on the reserves always with no exception welcome their people home. The people have great pride in the achievements of those who have been away and are always happy when they return.

There are even more people who come home and make a difference. The secret to success is to take their time. An ancient Native philosophy says *take your time*, and it means think things through, understand the problem first, do not be hasty, find the root of the problem. Successful returnees take the time to get to know the people and understand the way things work. They take the time to learn the reality of reserve living before using their wider knowable base for problem-solving. They eventually discover that the people on reserves are no different from anyone else, and the character flaws they were schooled about are a complete myth. Once they reach this awaking, they are usually able to make a difference. They will eventually learn that the difference they make is small, and oftentimes, temporary. No amount of education and dedication can change the underlying dysfunctional nature of Canada's reserve management regime created by successive Canadian governments.

The Glory Seekers and the Action Seekers

Two other reasons people run for council are either for the glory or simply to get in on the action. There is no glory or action to get into in stable pragmatic communities. It is the communities who have experienced windfalls and huge temporary increases in their own source revenue that attract the glory and action seekers. The glory seekers do little for the people, and instead spend their time promoting themselves outside the community. The glory of being on council is purely imaginary, and the imagination is emphasized and fueled by those who see a potential benefit. Staff and managers quickly learn that ego stroking is a far more profitable activity than production, resulting in severely diminished service delivery. Media and organizations cater to the glory seekers because of the publicity they can generate with exaggerated, sometime manufactured, progressive thinking and claiming the credit for the work of others. As with all ego-based glory, this all vanishes the day after losing an election.

The 'get in on the action' people generally try to stay under the radar. Their main objective is to enrich themselves and family members. Having a majority of 'get in on the action' people has proven to be the most destructive of all the types. A progressive and prosperous community can be turned into a have-not community in less than a year. Recovery can take years, and some communities never recover. The former councillors have little desire to take on the job of starting over, and former employees who made success possible have moved on.

CHAPTER 7:

Band Council Power and Powerlessness

Leadership is only leadership if there is power to lead.

The people who run for and get elected to band councils are first and foremost human beings. They have the same feelings, desires, flaws, strengths, and weaknesses common to all human beings everywhere. With a few exceptions, they are all good people trying to do an impossible job. They work under both a huge public misconception about what they have the power to do and an even greater misconception that comes from their members' belief of their powers.

There is no job description, rules or guidelines for band councils, and this causes a wide range of perceived powers. The one power they have is to determine what power they can exercise. Like most powers of band councils, it is not a real power but a power by default—meaning no one tells them they can't determine their own power, and no one is watching or required to watch. Most band council powers are powers by default.

Many of the people in most of the communities are fully aware of the powerlessness of band councils and have no desire to run or be involved in the running of the community. There are many more who run for other reasons ranging from a real desire to help to purely selfish reasons. Whatever the reason for running, winning generally changes the outlook of most people. Real training for band councils does not exist.

Two Views Travelling in Opposite Directions

Canadians are familiar with democratic forms of government and have a firm belief that FN people on reserves have the same privileges. Canadians are most familiar with mayors and city councils, school boards, health and hospital boards, regional districts, and their respective administrations. They are familiar with highway departments maintaining their roads, provincial health departments managing healthcare, provincial social services department providing assistance—though far from perfect—and social programs for the unfortunate. They know about the city or provincial police forces, the RCMP, Fish and Wildlife officers maintaining order and protecting citizens. The assumption of most Canadians is that everything that is available to them is also available to Indians on land reserved for Indians.

Not so.

It is beyond the scope of this book to attempt to examine and define the extent of the Canadian public's misconceptions about the Aboriginal people of Canada. The Canadian public's view reflected by Canadian writers and the Indigenous view reflected by Native writers are so different that they seem to be travelling in opposite directions. Reconciliation, whatever the term means, is an impossible task without fundamental changes in Canadian law. It would require a re-examining of the meaning and intent of section 91(24) of the Canadian Constitution. It is important to point out that the misconception began at confederation and continues to this day. There is no benefit to any government of Canada for the Canadian public to know the truth about the reality of Canada's Indigenous population. For governments, it is far more economical to allow misconceptions to continue indefinitely.

History of the Council

First Nations people also have a long list of misconceptions about the powers and responsibilities of their chiefs and councils. It is important to examine the people's view to have a clear understanding of the inner working of a community and the band administration. The band council system of government was designed by the British colonial powers long before confederation, and it was carried on by the new government of Canada. Through the work of anthropologists and religious organizations in the Americas, Africa, Australia, and other colonized countries, it was determined that all non-Europeans were tribal and could only operate in a tribal fashion.

With the creation of the Indian Act, the government of the day established band councils along the lines of what was believed to be a form of tribal government—defined by the anthropologists and religious leaders, and disguised as democracies by the band election requirements. The system was imposed on all bands in Canada with little resistance because government officials appointed the first band councils in a way that led the people to believe that their existing government system was being legitimized.

One of the devious methods was for Indian Agents to appoint what was referred to at the time as a favoured headman for chief councillor, and then appoint traditional leaders to council, giving the impression that the traditional leaders were being officially recognized. Reality set in once the requirement to hold elections was enforced and FN people have been demanding change ever since. Some have succeeded through modern day land claims agreements and self-government agreements, but the vast majority of FN communities are held firmly in place under the Indian Act by the capacity fallacy.

Council Powerlessness

The people living on reserves have no one besides the chief and council to turn to for anything—housing, good paying jobs, health, education, water, garbage collection and everything else a community in the twenty-first century needs to survive. The people have a belief that the councils can and should provide all the services needed. The truth is virtually all of the services come from either the Department of Indian and Norther Affairs or Health Canada. With growing populations and the cap on funding increase, the resources available to manage a Native community becomes smaller each year, and fewer and fewer people can be helped. Politics being politics, and as the financial resources shrink, it is the supporters of the council and program managers who are helped first, and the non-supporters are labeled disgruntled and are fed a steady diet of excuses. The favourite excuse used on the so-called disgruntled is *you are on the list*. There is no end of uses for that excuse.

The Canadian government departments do not concern themselves with the plight of individuals on reserves and rely entirely on the reports of staff and council. The belief that the council has the power to help them solve community problems, and the fact that they are always told all they have to do is wait, is the principle cause of individuals' powerlessness to help themselves.

The people are convinced by the councils that travelling and attending meetings are helping the community. People tend to believe the perpetual promise that chief and council attending meetings throughout the country will improve the living conditions on the reservation. The fact is that meetings are rarely productive and are simply part of the self-granted perks of being on council. There is no real need for councils to travel to meetings. Most meeting participants are simply observers and play no actual part and make no contribution to the discussions. The most successful band leaders in Canada are those who never travel and stay in their community and get work done. They only travel when there is a clear purpose. These stay-at-home leaders gain a clear understanding of their home community and can find innovative ways to make improvements to the lives of the people in their communities.

One of the reasons band members believe their council have the power and authority to take care of all their problems is the fact that the chief and council have almost dictatorial power over small things. Dictatorial in the sense that they do not need to concern themselves with what the people think, and the people have no power or process to appeal anything their council imposes on them. In other governments and organizations, this is known as micromanagement. On reserves, it is simply considered normal. That is the way it is, and with no appeal process available, no amount of complaining and protesting will make any difference.

Housing is one of the areas that councils have small dictatorial power. Councils have no control over the number of houses built or even where they are to be built. They have no control of the cost or size of homes, the mortgage rates, the mortgage terms, or rent charged. It is the Department of Indian and Northern Affairs and CMHC who hold and retain all these powers. A full explanation of the completely illogical system of providing Native housing in Canada would fill another volume.

Legal Nepotism

The one power the chief and councils have is who gets to live in the house. No other jurisdiction in the country has this power, only the chiefs and councils on reserves have this power. There are many across the country who take the power seriously and use it wisely. Some have policies to provide housing to those needing it the most. Some make sure the elders and families with small children are taken care of before anyone else. Some make a real effort to bring their people home to help grow and diversify their communities. Those dedicated people who make a real effort at making their people's lives better are paddling against the current. The Canadian Native housing system was not designed to do that.

The power to decide who gets to live in a house is wide open to abuse. The term abuse may not be the right term because it is not illegal for councils and staff to manipulate the system to their personal advantage. Any dictatorial power, large or small, comes with an almost irresistible temptation to make personal use of the power. The temptation commonly used is the election promise; the promise of a house can sway a lot of votes. After the election, promises can be kept by the simple delaying statement of *you're on the list.*

Because resources on reserves are so limited, councils tend to take care of family members ahead of everyone else. Often, they take care of themselves. It is important to remember these things don't usually happen because people are corrupt or dishonest. It happens because it is legal. Chiefs and councils controlling the lives of individuals is not only legal in Canada, but also required by the laws and policies of the government in keeping with the communal fallacy.

Post-secondary educations have rules and guidelines created by the policy-makers that the chief and staff are required to follow. Like all rules and guidelines in band administration, there is no monitoring of whether they are being followed.

The department relies on the reports sent in by the staff to monitor implementation. This loose monitoring leaves room for nepotism and favouritism and the ever-present election promise. Most staff have the best interest of the student in mind and try to make the best decisions to help the most students. Since the best interests of the chief and council usually end up being paramount to everything else, staff dedication can be perilous to job security.

The chief and individual council members and some staff members make sure their family members are taken care of first. This is not done because of corruption; it is done because it is possible under the department's education system. Band members who complain to the council or staff are told that they are just following policy. Members who complain directly to the department are referred to staff and council. Chiefs and councils have no real legislated or delegated power; their power comes from the futility of any attempt at appealing their decisions. The complete absence of any available remedy for the people, coupled with the absence of individual rights, is what gives the councils the perception of dictatorial powers. It is not that the councils have dictatorial powers, it is that there is an absence of controls on council's powers. Complaints of abuses by staff and council to the government of Canada are generally referred back to the staff and council, who can then claim they are just disgruntled members.

Hiring and Firing

Before the Canada Labour Code was applied to reserves, every election meant a wholesale firing of anyone who did not support nor were related to the new chief councillor. The labour code discourages rather than prevents this from happing today, but it still happens. It happens slowly, but it happens. Councils and loyal staff can always find ways to justify letting "disgruntled" or "troublemaking" staff members go.

This condition has an extremely negative effect on the community because staff with the hammer of council over their heads have only two options in this case. First is to do as little as possible in the hope of surviving until the next election. And second is to continue doing the best they can until they are driven out. Councils can eliminate the position, cut off funding, fabricate complaints against the employee, or simply treat the employee so badly they give up and quit. Very few people file a complaint to Labour Canada because the councils can punish complaining band members in other ways. Councils may have reduced firing powers, but they still have dictatorial hiring powers.

Councils control hiring in various ways. One way is making a rule that a hiring committee be all council members. If committees are not council members, the committee members are all council appointees. A band manager or CEO can also assume the arbitrary powers of the chief councillor; it is not a legal power but merely a convenient method of keeping non-supporters out of the office. No other jurisdiction in the country allows elected politicians to be directly involved in the hiring of employees to prevent nepotism and conflict of interest. On Canada's Indian reservations, it is not only legal, but it is the norm.

An Absence of Rules

The problems that exist on the reserves exist because of an absence of rules. When rules are created, they are usually made by staff and consultants. In every case, the rules are slanted to benefit the staff and council. Consultants generally have little or no knowledge of local conditions. They utilize standard templates used in other communities that they have worked for, or in some cases, push their own ideas to enhance their earning power in future projects. Standard templates rarely, if ever, work in FN communities.

There is no known attempt by any government to examine or find and implement real solutions that will benefit the people living on the reserves. Band councils, and provincial and national Native leaders are equally at fault in the failure to fix the problem because of the existing principle of *if it is good for the band members, it is bad for the chief and council, and if it is good for the chief and council, it is bad for the people.* The principle is a fact. Band councillors are human beings the same as anyone else, and if there is the power to choose options, human nature will choose the option most desirable to the human doing the choosing. Canadians are under the mistaken belief that Indian band management dysfunction is caused by the character flaw created by official policy. They believe that the dysfunction is because they are Indians, and that is just the way Indians are. No one has made any attempt to disabuse them of this belief.

Bands across the country have all at one time or another attempted to find solutions to the difficulties of band management. Solutions—no matter how effective—function because of the complete lack of due process under the Indian Act. The life of the solutions last only as long as the life of the council that created them. The lack of due process means a new council can simply ignore the rules and create their own or have no rules at all.

Council Power

Much has been written about the authority of band councils to govern their communities. First Nations' courses in colleges and universities, INAC sponsored workshops, workshops by self-declared experts, lawyers, and all manners of people all list and teach the powers and responsibilities of being on band council. What they do not teach is that none of it is of any use. Systems and procedures developed in the nineteenth century have no relevance in the twenty-first century.

Under the Indian Act, the bands can propose laws but do not have the authority to enact laws. All band bylaws need the approval, or what can be termed the non-disapproval, of the minister. All proposed bylaws are sent to the department, and if there is no response after forty-five days, the law is considered to be in effect. The bylaws are reviewed by a Department of Justice lawyer, and more often than not, the law is denied for exceeding Indian Act authority. Very few bands make bylaws for their communities since the powers listed in the Indian Act are powers that may have been useful one hundred years ago but have little application in the twenty-first century. Laws made by councils on reserves are virtually impossible to enforce anyway, so there is little or no consequence to ignoring the law. On reserve ignorance of the law is an excuse. Neither the RCMP, Canadian prosecutors, nor the courts enforce Indian band laws.

In the past number of years, through the dedicated effort of small groups of bands, some federal laws have been passed for specific purposes. The Land Management Act (LMA) and the First Nations Fiscal Management Act (FNFMA) work well for the bands that originally proposed them because the acts were designed to work with specific problems in those communities. As is the case in towns and municipalities across Canada, what works in one place does not always work in another.

A major problem with these specific purpose laws is not what is in them but what is missing. The federal laws delegate lawmaking powers to the bands in specific sectors, such as managing Indian reserve lands owned by the government of Canada, but they are still Indian Act band councils with the same limitations imposed by the Indian Act. The laws they make under the acts are not Canadian enactments. This means they are not Canadian laws and are not part of the Canadian legal system.

Indian Act band councils were never intended nor designed to be legislators or law-making bodies. Because the band councils do not have resources to develop laws matching local issues, the usual procedure is to off load the responsibility to managers.

Under the Indian Act, chief and councils and the staff do all the things they do directly with whatever authority they believe they have and whatever they can get away with without having to make laws. Many band councils under the LMA and FNFMA carry on the tradition of rule by personal opinion rather than making actual laws. Bands cannot be faulted for bypassing the law-making step because neither the Indian Act nor the LMA and FNFMA establishes any form of local legislative institution. The federal institutions have rules of conduct, but there is no way to monitor or enforce the rules. Bands can make laws but have nothing like the bylaw-making procedures used by municipalities. The usual result is to delegate the law-making process to the lands manager, giving the lands manager personal power over the members in land matters.

When staff can draft laws and policies that they will work under, they will without exception draft the laws and policies to their advantage. There are actual cases where staff have given themselves more authority than the council and have even used that authority to discipline council members who disagree. This peculiar staff power happens when the chief personally benefits from the staff having control over the council because to fix the problem all that is required is to fire the responsible staff member. And as long as the staff member keeps the chief councillor happy, they can stay in control.

CHAPTER 8:

Continuity and Consequences

Knowledge is power, withholding knowledge is an even greater power.

The operation of Indian Act band councils has remained basically unchanged for the past fifty years. A new council simply starts meeting without a process of transition from one council to the next. Since most council decisions are made by a council motion with a show of hands and not by law, none of the decisions made by previous councils have any effect on the new council. Other established governments have procedures to rescind or amend decisions of predecessors along with the responsibility of public servants to inform government members of all decisions of their predecessors and the consequences of ignoring past decisions. Under the Indian Act, there are no such procedures; motions made by previous councils are simply ignored as if they never existed. There is nothing in the Indian Act or any other Canadian law requiring continuity. New councils pretty much start from scratch. Every new council creates an uncertainty in the staff, and they usually sit back until they determine the mood of the new council.

Building on the Past

There are some communities who have made an effort toward governing continuity. Continuity in this case can be defined to mean building on past action, making constant improvements in band management, and building internal institutions for orderly management. Governing continuity requires ignoring the Indian Act and creating lasting progressive policy that focuses on improving the way of life in their home communities.

This can only be carried out by progressive thinkers in a community because in the absence of any regulatory body, it can only be as good as the people managing the policy. Under the Indian Act, changes or improvement can only be accomplished using the band's internal policy, and policy can be either ignored or changed at the stroke of a pen. Because policy can only be enforced by the same people who wrote the policy, when a new inexperienced council begins, they view the existing policy as the old council's policy not theirs and start over again.

Councils and staff who have learned through experience about the nonsensical and illogical nature of federal laws and policies governing Native communities will simply ignore the laws and policies and create their own. Those with experience know that the bureaucrats at the federal government are basically good-hearted people and will look the other way because many of them agree that the laws and policies make little sense in the current world. On the other hand, inexperienced staff and councils, who are not familiar with the realities of band management, tend to work by the book. And in most cases, if replacing a progressive group, this can and often does set the band back fifty years. Inexperienced councils are pretty much at the mercy of the staff and the consultants they hire to teach them. Progress without external checks and balances cannot be sustained. Bands under the Indian Act will always, without fail, revert to the average when the progressive leaders are replaced. The system is self-correcting. The default average created by Canadian government laws and policy is "mediocrity."

No Enforceable Checks and Balances

Democracy cannot function without enforceable checks and balances. The key word is "enforceable." The governments of Canada whether they be federal, provincial, or municipal, all have checks and balances imbedded in law and convention. Repercussions for wrongdoing fall on the wrongdoer in all levels of government in Canada except band councils under the Indian Act. Wrongdoers are never punished; it is the band members who are punished for the misdeeds of their leaders and staff. They are punished by the Department of Indian and Northern Affairs by way of all their funding being cut off. This means: stopping all services such as education, social services, road maintenance, and any other services relied on by any other community in Canada. The long-standing Canadian policy is one of the effects of the communal fallacy.

Democratic governments are ultimately accountable to the people who elected them. They are held accountable by parliament and watchdogs, the auditor general, opposition parties, the legitimate media, world opinion, and ultimately, by the voter. In a democracy, there are penalties in law and convention for misdeeds while being part of government. There is evidence for this in the number of prime ministers and provincial premiers who have had to resign in Canada for exercising poor judgment. These MPs, MLAs or senators are ejected from their parties, charged or forced to resign. All of them pay the price for forgetting or ignoring democratic accountability. Whether the misdeeds were intentional, well-meaning, or accidental—the price is the same.

The councils are not accountable to the people, they are accountable to the Minister of Indian Affairs or his/her agents. Because band elections are held every two years, it is accurate to say that band councils members are accountable to the people who elect them for one day every two years. Once the election is over, the accountability to the people function is fulfilled and is set aside for another two years. Many people, including lawyers and consultants, say that this is merely a technical argument and that councils are ultimately accountable to the band members voting in elections. Except in cases of extreme misbehaviour, voting in a band election is more of a popularity contest than an accountability exercise.

The Native people of Canada, whether living on the reserves or elsewhere in Canada, have no penalties available to them for council or staff's misdeeds or neglect of duty. The standard community joke is "if we all disappeared, the staff and council wouldn't even notice." There is no penalty for failure to report to the people. There is no penalty for feeding the people false information or reports. There is no penalty for presenting misleading financial information. There is also no penalty for the band staff misleading the council or the people.

The people are powerless.

On the other hand, the Department of Indian Affairs, Health Canada and any other federal or provincial government require countless reports. Some require monthly reports, some require quarterly reports, and all require annual reports. Government and industry control the councils with the purse strings through reports. No report? No further funding. To repeat, reports are not used to check on the progress of the band members but simply to fulfill the reporting requirements of the bureaucracy. If they can be filed, further funding can be processed.

Even if a band creates checks and balances or reporting requirements for themselves, there is no way under any Canadian law which will allow for enforcement of the checks and balances beyond the life of the council creating them.

Freedom of the Press?

In Canada, the media, also known as the fifth estate, keeps a constant eye on the activities of governments and are free to write whatever they believe to be true. One of the major checks on the powers of government is media doing their job along with good editorial policy. Without the good, honest media operating freely, corrupt government controlling public information can function with impunity. Freedom of the press is one of the major cornerstones of democracy.

On Canada's reserves, there is no freedom of the press. Those who argue that this is not possible in a country like Canada have never lived under the iron thumb of band staff and council. Controlling all communications is one of the unwritten powers of staff and council. It must be understood that there is no actual power over communications; the real power comes from the absence of any powers or willingness by the powers that be to say otherwise. Freedom of speech is a part of the Canadian Constitution, and the freedom actually exists and is protected by the courts in Canada. However, that freedom is suspended on the reservations by the silence of the government of Canada.

Suppression of freedoms on reserves is possible because of the Canadian public's belief in a different reality for Indians of Canada. The notion that it is like that because they are Indians and Indians are supposed to be treated like that runs deep in Canada. Band and Indian organization leaders prefer to keep it that way because controlling information going to the people is one of their most powerful tools in maintaining their public stations. It is the main reason FN leaders have fought to keep Indian bands and the people exempt from the application of the Human Rights Act.

Individual band members have had little success in breaking through the freedom barrier. There have been a few who have been successful in publishing misbehaviour, but the personal cost can be very high. To begin with, the chief and council control communications by keeping any newsletters band-owned. Any staff member writing anything appearing to be critical of the chief and council members will undoubtedly end up standing in the unemployment line. Only nice things about the chief and council are permitted to be written. Any attempt by band members to create a factual paper is immediately set upon by staff, lawyers, and consultants whose instruction from the chief is to discredit and marginalize the culprit. If the member is a band employee, a reason is quickly found to dissolve the position. If the person is not an employee, then policy is created to make the person ineligible for any position. All of it is done legally due to the absence of rules and laws. Band members complaining to the department officials about the suppression of their freedom of speech are always without exception considered an internal matter and of no concern to the government of Canada. There is no record found of the Human Rights Commission ever taking up a case of suppression of rights on any reserve in Canada.

The local mainstream media has a built-in reluctance to print band members' complaints regarding any wrongdoing on the part of council and band staff. Local papers rely on band advertising for much of their revenue. Good relations between the local paper and chief and council are a good source of news items to keep small papers interesting. Individual members bringing wrongdoing stories to local papers generally go nowhere because the reporters will call the chief or manager for confirmation, which in turn triggers the general quarters response. Staff, lawyers, and consultants immediately begin enter the supress, discredit and marginalize mode, and the story dies. Members know that attempting to go public is a waste of time and do not bother. The democratic instrument of the freedom of the press is nonexistent for the Native people of Canada. Again, it is because Canadians believe *it is because they are Indians, and that is how Indians are supposed to be treated,* and this is all quite legal in Canada.

Saved by the Media

The Indian Act does not establish or create a band council in a band. What the Act does in regard to band councils is to establish the power of the minister to declare by ministerial order the election of a chief and council.

Clause 74(1) of the Indian Act reads: *Whenever he deems it advisable for the good government of a band, the minister may declare by order that after a day to be named therein the council of the band, consisting of a chief and councillors, shall be selected by elections to be held in accordance with this Act.*

The Act does not provide for any controls or instruction on how chief and councils are to operate, nor does it mention anything about the role of band managers. Band councils under the Indian Act exist at the pleasure of the minister and have no real powers of their own; they are set up to be advisors to the minister. The Act has created a paradox by not allowing councils to have real powers, but at the same time, not subjecting councils to any controls on what they do.

By staying under the radar and out of the public eye, band councils can get away with just about anything. The people living on the reserves have no powers or processes available to them to hold their chief and councillors accountable. As long as the mainstream media can be kept silent, councils are free to do as they please. Complaints by community members to the department are simply referred by the media back to the band council.

Third-Party Management

Since the beginning of the transfer of responsibility, the government of Canada has taken a hands-off policy in the internal affairs of bands and look the other way when community members make complaints. Even though there is an allegations and complaints section within the department, it is only concerned with the misuse of department funds and election procedure violations. The department only steps in when misdeeds become public and the department is made to look bad. Because the councils exist at the pleasure of the minister, the power the minister uses to express displeasure is third-party management. Third-party management removes all powers from the chief and council and places the authority on a manager hired by the department and paid for with the band's money. The equivalent of a third-party manager in the rest of Canada is the receiver in bankruptcy.

The principle behind the third-party management policy is that Canada does not accept responsibility and has no reason or intent to correct internal problems; their only role is to manage at the band's expense. Chief and council are not removed as councillors; only their authority and responsibilities are taken over. They continue all of their activities and still receive all the perks, but the third-party manager makes all of the decisions. The manager assumes full control of everything in the band, including lawmaking, policy-making, hiring and firing, and financial management. The manager reports to the department and has no requirement to report to the people. And the people have no way to appeal the decisions of the third-party manager. The third-party manager does not replace the council and staff; the manager simply becomes their ruler with full arbitrary power.

CHAPTER 9:

Discontinuity—Transitions, Meetings, and Record-Keeping

When the people's lives are governed by someone other than themselves, meetings are constant.

Transitions

All governments with any degree of democracy pay great attention during the transition from one government to the next. Without a good transition process, stability in governing is not possible.

Dictatorships don't need transitions; they simply start dictating.

Bands are neither governments with real governing powers nor are they dictatorships. Because of the nature of the job, they still should have a transition process but don't, and none is required by anyone. Bands are allowed by the department to behave as if they were governments as long as they stay in line. Band councils are still structured as they were envisioned by European governments one hundred and fifty years ago. The appearance and circumstances may be different, but it is the same structure.

Europeans pictured chiefs sitting in a circle discussing and ruling on everyday issues of immediate concern using only their collective wisdom. This is a fairly accurate picture of the old way of governing before contact. Wisdom came from experience—leaders were trained from childhood, and each leader was a specialist in their field. A civilization without written information required specialists from all the fields that the community was involved in, such as farmers, engineers and construction workers, geographers, artists, entertainers, doctors, planners, historians, and numerous others. Every major decision required the leaders to bring in a specialist for advice. The specialists were the books—with a lifetime of training and experience, they were the equivalent to the people who hold PhDs today. The key to the success of the old system was continuity; the wisdom and knowledge, old and new, was constantly being brought forward generation after generation. The Indian Act adopted the structure but not the underlying principles behind the old system of governance.

A new council begins the day after the election, and there is no requirement for an orderly transition. There are bands who attempt to ensure there is some form of continuity, but without enforceable rules or laws, transition is at the pleasure of the new council. A new council whose members strongly oppose the outgoing council generally prefer to wipe the board clean and start as if the previous council never existed.

The old method of ensuring the continuity of wisdom and experience has been erased, not by deliberately outlawing it, but by the Indian Act and its regulations remaining silent during time of transition.

Record-Keeping

Fifty years ago, before the devolution of band management, continuity was the responsibility of the Indian Agent. The Indian Agent had at his disposal a large bureaucracy of record-keepers. At the beginning of the devolution exercise, the bands were handed responsibilities and simply told *this is yours now* without assistance of any kind. No band complained about the responsibility; everyone without exception was happy to see less of the Indian Agent. Regardless of the struggle, no band would ever even consider bringing back the meddlesome Indian Agent. They would much rather develop their own bureaucracies as best they can.

The mountain of records produced by the federal bureaucracy remain in archives scattered across the country, and these archives are not available to the bands they refer to. Requests for historic information usually receive the response that there are no department staff available to even find the location of the files, never mind go through the files.

No system has been devised by the government of Canada or any Indian Act band on an effective method of keeping records. A file clerk in government is a dedicated person who is required to do routine tasks like data entry, organization, cross-referencing, scanning, copying and retrieval. Legal file clerks are responsible for following a filing system and organizing records, such as letters, legal documents, case files, correspondence, invoices and memoranda according to that system. They locate and retrieve requested files, as well as prepare legal document indices, file folders and labels. Bands do not have the resources to have a full-time file/legal clerk on staff, nor is there any training available to any employee. Making funding available for training will not solve the training problem because no one has ever analyzed the actual record-keeping requirement of bands. Colleges, schools, and training consultants teach the same filing methods.

Most band filing systems are designed to put documents away out of sight, but little attention is paid to retrieving needed documents. In almost all cases, document retrieval depends on the same individual who filed it, and so the system relies on that person's memory. If there is staff turnover and documents are needed, the method is to go through everything until it is found, or contact the people who sent it and get a copy. The principle of record-keeping in a band office is mainly individual staff preference. Bands generally receive large amounts of daily mail, 90% of which has little to do with the operation of the band. E-mail is pretty much impossible to keep track of, let alone finding a way to put e-mails into a filing system.

Each time there is a new manager or senior staff change, the record-keeping system changes. Under the Indian Act, nothing in the operation of the band can be made permanent. Bands who have tried central filing systems have found that it will work for a while, and then begins to fall apart as time goes on and new people take over. Confidential material is never secure in a central filing system. The same problem of a lack of enforceable rules, standards or regulation on record-keeping practically ensures any system will eventually become useless.

Any attempt to solve the problem with the help of the Department of Indian and Northern Affairs usually involves hiring consultants approved by the department and usually ends up being designed for the wrong purpose. Consultants always without fail come with preconceived plans on the design of a record-keeping system. Consultants, by the nature of their business, come with very narrow views and use information supplied by the department's bureaucracy. They will design an elaborate central system (including cross-referencing along with policy manuals) that requires a full-time filing expert to operate. Any system that is not designed to fit the normal way people do things will very quickly fail once the consultant is paid and leaves. None of the methods devised by consultants includes a systematic process to provide information for accountability to the members. Allowing access to selective information can never be called accountability.

Small Reserves Need Simple Systems

Elaborate systems never work for long because they are designed for reasons that no one in the community has ever had any need for. One very elaborate record-keeping system designed by the department policy experts was the infrastructure management and tracking system for the maintenance of community assets. Systems designed to operate in municipalities of 30,000 people with huge public works budgets do not work well on small Indian reserves with little or no budget to work with. Maintenance workers complained that the paperwork took up most of their time, leaving far less time to do the work of maintaining community assets. A far better system would have been a calendar on the wall with tasks scheduled in, and requiring a weekly walk around the community to see what needs fixing—that is all that is really needed. Consultants and career bureaucrats fight tooth and nail to avoid simple systems. Elaboration is their bread and butter; the more elaborate, the more bread and butter.

Robert's Rules

Record-keeping in a band is far more than filing and retrieving correspondence. Records of decisions come in various forms, and each form is kept differently. Decisions made in a council meeting are done by someone moving a motion after an issue is discussed and seconded by someone, and then voted on. Robert's

Rules of Order are never followed as they are in municipal councils. Each community band council simply does whatever works for them. Robert's Rules of Order require a motion to be tabled on an issue before it can be discussed, and any changes be made by motions to amend. Councils consider Robert's Rules to be far too cumbersome and unnecessary. For Indian Act band councils with little or no powers, this is true. They simply discuss an issue, and once some agreement is reached, someone proposes a motion and it is seconded. If there further discussion and/or changes to the motion need to be made, the mover and seconder agree to the change, and then the motion is voted on and is either passed or defeated. The motion is recorded in the minutes and that is the only place it is recorded. Staff are rarely if ever informed of the decision, and there is no requirement to make the minutes available to the members. Most council decisions do not have anything to do with the well-being of the members, and councils have no compelling reason to inform them of something that has nothing to do with them. For example, band members never hear of council's policy of paying themselves additional honourariums while travelling.

Band Council Resolutions

Band Council Resolutions (BCRs) are written documents required under the Indian Act. They are statements of a band council's intent or consent, and they are signed by a majority of council members. BCRs and resolutions made in council meetings are not the same thing. BCRs are required by government departments to indicate majority approval of something. Since they are not legal documents, they do not bind anyone. Governments use them as proof they are not acting without consent. No provisions in the act have been made to retroactively rescind BCRs, even though band managers and their lawyers go through the motions of rescinding old BCRs in the belief they are binding and have legal standing. The intent of previous councils cannot be rescinded and made void retroactively, only the policy intent of the current council can be recorded in a BCR. BCRs are sent to whichever government department or funding organization requires them. Bands do not actually need BCRs for internal purposes, but most bands will use them as if they were legal instruments. All that is required for action is the motion in the minutes. Each council places different importance on BCRs. Some have meticulous records and files for BCRs, while others simply send them off to whoever needs them and then let staff do whatever they want with the rest. Band members never see BCRs unless they are personally affected by them.

Staff Meetings Are to Run the Office, not the Community

There are as many external meetings, workshops, training programs and conventions for chiefs, councillors, and staff as there are working days in a year. Over 90% of the meetings scheduled and attended serve no purpose other than to fuel the meeting industry. Successful leaders have made it a point to only attend the 5% that are actually useful and make a difference.

The endless schedule of meetings is a direct result of the capacity fallacy. The government of Canada, the provinces and Indian organizations spend millions on group personal development workshops and training programs for band staff and band councils, all of which involve long-distance travel. A three-day workshop, for example, means an extra two travel days with pay and expenses. Council members and staff enjoy the five days away from the community as a way to avoid the day-to-day community nuisances. Many of the staff are non-Native and many are not members of the band, so there is no net benefit to the community to train employees who will never be part of the community. Many will argue that the training of band staff, regardless of who they are, is a benefit to the community, but as with any fallacy argument, it is a rationalization rather than a fact.

There is no requirement for the chief, councillors or staff to provide meeting reports to anyone. Minutes are not kept on the majority of the meetings and workshops. Reports are usually done by the meeting sponsors and are always filled with glowing reports of the success of the gathering—success can be manufactured when necessary. The people at the community are never told of the meetings or the results of the meetings. Social media is sometimes the only window the people have into the comings and goings of the people they elected and hired to run their lives.

A good band staff meeting happens when community issues are discussed and a plan of action involving all band office departments and any external service providers work together to find and implement solutions. Band council minutes and instructions should be reviewed for any new instructions or new directions. A well-functioning staff requires constant feedback from the community they are hired to manage. Without recorded feedback, the administration staff eventually becomes self-serving.

For feedback from the people living in the community to be effective and useful for the staff and band council, staff meeting objectives must be to measure how effective is the service delivery to the community. Because of the line dividing the people in the community and council and staff, none of this ever happens. The band staff's main concern in band staff meetings is the running of the office, not the running of the community.

Most band staff meetings are similar to office meetings held by businesses and are mainly about the running of the office. They are called for staff discipline, determining holiday times, the latest schedules, and other such routine matters. No pre-planning is done, no objectives are established before the meeting, and no records other than personal notes of participants are recorded or kept. Most band staff meetings are called because it's thought of as a good idea, and a report can be made to council that a staff meeting was held. No records are kept and no follow-up is ever needed. A standard band staff meeting is the staff giving, one by one, verbal reports to each other. If the objective is to call a staff meeting and have everyone make a report, then if everyone shows up and makes a report, the meeting objective has been met. Anyone who attends these meetings is aware that no one listens to anyone else's report. The main concern of each participant is to dream up some clever lines for their own report. Once their report is presented, there is no real need to pay attention to anyone else's report.

In the Age of Personal Computers

Before the coming of the personal computer and instant communications, all of the paperwork was carried out by secretaries. These secretaries were trained to write and keep track of all documents and were the experts in information management. The personal computer has made the job of the secretary obsolete. Every staff member is supplied with their own computer and writes their own letters, emails, and anything else that needs to be written.

For a band, this created two major problems. The first is record-keeping since little correspondence is printed for the file, and so filing cabinets and central filing systems are quickly becoming obsolete. All staff keep their own files, usually in one of their desk drawers. E-mails are rarely printed and filed and are kept instead in the computers for safekeeping. The problem with keeping information in a computer is computers become obsolete every three to five years and must be replaced. Many of the programs in the old computers will not work with the new systems, so much of the files are lost, particularly if the files were archived in the old computer. Many 32-bit files will not open with the 64-bit system used in all computers today.

Again, the problem with filing is the economics of scale, whether it is the old filing systems or electronic systems. 90% of the bands are too small to make use of a comprehensive filing system, and no one has made any attempt to design a workable system. Hiring consultants or trainers always results in the same outcome. Consultants will always install an overdesigned system. This happens to the point where the filing system drives the operation of the office, and the only solution is to stop using it and go back to the haphazard *everyone for themselves* method.

Democratic government requires continuity. Good, orderly, and consistent record-keeping is essential to maintaining continuity because continuity requires controls and penalties on both the outgoing council and the new council. It also requires band management controls and penalties for failure to act honestly and openly.

CHAPTER 10:

Problematic Solutions

The roots of discriminative FN policy in Canada run deep

In my work through the years trying to understand the root cause of these impediments, obstacles and barriers, I have found it best to make use of philosophical principles to put into useful perspective some of the main unsolvable inequities in Native communities.

The Latin term *petitio principii*, or begging the question; is logically valid but unpersuasive in that it fails to prove anything other than what is already assumed. More simply put: the answer is in the question. If someone were given the *Jeopardy* answer "because they are Indians," almost any question that includes the word Indians would be correct. Question: Why are Indian reserves so poorly managed? Answer: Because they are Indians. Question: Why is there a housing crisis on the reserves? Answer: Because they are Indians. Canadians, including First Nations people and their leaders, have a belief that the Native people in Canada live in a different reality, and that the reason Native people are treated differently from all the other people of Canada is "because they are Indians."

The belief that Indians must be treated differently is at its strongest in government. All the people in national and provincial government departments, including Native leaders, firmly believe it is not possible to treat Indians the same as anyone else. Even the mere suggestion of having the existing provincial delivery institutions (such as school boards and provincial social services infrastructure) deliver education, health and basic social services to Native people is seen by the Native leaders as an attack on the equilibrium of their power.

The reason is not for any racist reason or lack of knowledge but because of how section 91(24) of the Canadian Constitution is interpreted. The Constitution of Canada does not require discrimination, nor was discrimination contemplated against Aboriginal people, but official discrimination is how it has always been interpreted. Maintaining the current interpretation is one of the most profitable opportunities for lawyers and consultants. Major law and consulting firms have been built on the notion that Indians must be treated differently, and correcting the misconception would be bad for business.

The editorial policies in the mainstream media are the worst offenders, especially in the terms they use. One example is the use of the word "hostile" by the CBC in a recent news item regarding Native opposition to the gas pipelines. A report of a missing person anywhere in Canada is a major news story and triggers a massive public search response by concerned citizens. If the story is about a missing Aboriginal, there is no massive public search response because the story is not about a person missing but about another Aboriginal missing. It is normal practice for reporters to group missing persons into two categories: persons and Aboriginals. The reason: because they are Indians. Editorial policy sees no problem in a headline about a statement made by an Indigenous lawyer, but see a headline about a statement made by a Caucasian lawyer as a racist problem.

The housing problem is another example: the media never tells the audience that all of the houses on reserves are owned by the government of Canada because Indians on reserves are not allowed by the Indian Act to own land on the reserve. There is a misconception that only Indian men can own their homes—of course, this is not true because no one can own a home on a reserve. The Canadian public is never told that a person making improvements to a house on a reserve adds no equity for the person living on it. The reporters and news writers are not to be blamed for the different view of Native peoples in Canada; the vast majority of writers do not intend to be racists. They write what they write because that is how it has always been done.

Editorial boards or independent editors all set the standard of their respective publications and news outlets, and the standard has always been to use certain terms when the news is about Aboriginal people. Treating Aboriginal people differently from other Canadians is legal in Canada, beginning with the interpretation of the constitution to the Indian Act to the Department of Indian Affairs to the media and the citizens of Canada.

Devolving responsibility vs. devolving authority

In the 1960s, the government of Canada began turning over financial management and band administration, some of the functions of the Department of Indian and Northern Affairs, to the bands. It was the beginning of a planned process to devolve responsibility to band councils. The process attempted to deal with the problem of capacity in the devolution implementation. The old assumption that the collective intelligence of Native people was below the collective intelligence of their neighbours persisted and played a major role in the failure of the process. Rather than focusing on creating better systems of management, the focus was and continues to be on improving the character of the Indian. The theory being that responsibility and management authority is withheld by the government of Canada until the Native people reach a level of development acceptable to the bureaucrats who created the devolution process. No one has yet figured out that spending millions of dollars on a problem that does not exist results in never finding a solution regardless of the effort.

There is no question that the governments and national and provincial Native organizations are well-intentioned and believe the solutions they come up with will work.

So why haven't they worked?

Opposing Views

There is no single reason for the failure to improve living conditions for Native people. The main problem guaranteeing failure for the people living on the reserves is the two opposing views: the Canadian public's view and the view from the reserves. When efforts are viewed by the Canadian public, it appears to them that the government is doing far too much for the ungrateful Indians. Most Canadians believe there is a simple solution to the Indian problem—all the Indians have to do is stop being Indians and do what we do.

When viewed by the Indians living on the reserves, the same efforts are viewed as meaningless or just more money for the band office to spend. The view of the Canadian public is the one that policy developers use to come up with what they see as solutions. The Indian population's view when seen by the policy people is always heavily coloured by the brown lens of public perception. It is the policy developers who decide what problems need solving, and that view is not the Indian view, resulting in misdirected objectives that may satisfy the Canadian observer and the voters, but creates zero results in Native communities.

The actions taken by most Canadian governments are to solve specific problems or to satisfy the Canadian voter. Actions and programs are created with specific objectives. No matter the objective, they never seem to have any positive effect on the lives of Native people on reserves.

Collateral Problem-Solving

One reason that proposed solutions do not work is the "collateral problem-solving" objective. The focus is a problem or symptom created by the actual problem. Many of the remedies devised by policy-makers have nothing to do with improving the lives of Native people. Most initiatives are about reducing costs in the federal budget. The policy of the 2% cap on the growth of the department budget is an example of cost cutting. The initiative narrative surrounding the cap was Native people were being taught to gradually raise their own revenue, but the initiative did not include the transfer of the authority to raise revenue, nor did it consider the fact that the vast majority of northern communities have no possible source of revenue in any case. The result of the initiative is that Native communities in Canada are far worse off than they were before the initiative. And even more money is now needed to repair the damage caused by the 2% cap. This is a classic case of an initiative having the opposite result of the intended outcome.

The solution to contaminated water is an advisory to boil the water.

The turning over of the administration of health care and education to Native-run organizations is primarily a cost-saving measure. The programs are transfered to Native control, but the administrative portion of the program is withheld by the government. Thus, there is a huge amount of savings for the government but an added burden on the people. The Conservative party proposed an education legislation. It was strenuously opposed because it was designed to wash the hands of the federal government, and at the same time, garner huge savings in administration costs. Almost all devolutionary steps are hindered by the collateral problem-solving objective. Collateral problem-solving happens for two main reasons. First, it is far easier to work on the symptoms. And second, it appears to the public that something is being done.

Political Problem-Solving

A second reason solutions don't work is the "political problem-solving" objective. Political parties in power sometimes need to move some obstacle or annoying problem to the side to satisfy some segment of their constituents. The Conservative's First Nations Financial Transparancy Act is an example of political problem-solving. The act required that the salaries of elected officials be posted on the internet, and if they did not post the numbers, funding for the entire band would be cut off. The act required punishing the band members by withholding money due to them if their elected leaders and their staff refused to follow the law. The act provided no punishment for the actual offenders. The act made the Conservative base and the Canadian taxpayer associations happy, but did nothing to address the FN people's need for accountability. Instead of making the elected leaders accountable to the people, the act made them accountable by law to the bureaucracy holding the purse strings. The act gave the department the power of judge and executioner. The act made no improvement to leaders' accountability, but that was never the intention of the bill. The bill served its purpose of gaining votes from the base and good press in showing the Canadian public something has been done.

Another example of political problem-solving is the Conservative plan to allow Native women to own homes on reserves to help solve the matrimonial dispute problem. The public outcry of the battered women created a political need to do something to help Native women and their children on reserves to avoid becoming homeless in a matrimonial dispute. The problem is real and since provincial family laws do not apply on Indian reserves, and no attempt is made to enforce the law on reserves, the communities have no remedy available to them to solve a very real problem. In a matrimonial dispute, the RCMP is called, but the only law they can enforce is the criminal code law against violence. If no one is being physically injured, they consider the problem contained, and the dispute simply becomes just another Indian problem.

The police and the courts do not consider laws made by Native bands to be enactments of laws in Canada, and thus these laws are routinely ignored. In Canada, laws made by Indian bands have no more legal standing in the Canadian judicial system than the bylaws of a nonprofit society.

The problem with the Conservative plan was that it was intended to make it appear that something had been done to work toward a solution, when in fact it was a poorly thought-out plan. As stated earlier, men can't own their homes on reserves either. The Indian Act does not allow anyone to own land on reserves. The Indian Act only allows Native people to use and occupy land, never to own the land.

Reserves are federal lands owned by the government of Canada. The public is generally unaware no one can own land on a reserve, and the reporters reporting the story simply write what they assume to be true. It makes a much better media story and great political hay to blame Indian men. There is no way to know if the public is being deliberately misled or whether the politicians making these announcements are badly misinformed.

New Air Filter Solution

The third reason solutions do not work is the "new air filter" problem-solving objective. This entails finding a solution that is designed to clean the air, remove some of the objections, and take care of the unpopular current view of the problem. The solution is designed to make it appear that the problem is taken seriously and is being worked on, when in fact it is not. An example is the Harper apology on the residential school issue. The apology solved the appearance that the Harper government did not concern themselves with Indigenous people. There was never any intention to do anything more. The apology gave comfort to the residential school victims and created the illusion something great was underway.

History records there were no further plans to do anything more, and no plans to change the education system designed a century ago. The Minister of Indian Affairs still has the power, under the Indian Act, to decide where Native children go to school. The residential schools have been replaced by the boarding program, where children are removed from their communities and brought to boarding homes in southern communities to attend school. The reason the policy persists is the government of Canada is saving money by not having to build and operate high schools in northern Native communities.

Provinces routinely build and operate high schools for northern and isolated communities. The right to an education in the provinces excludes Native children. The provinces annually collect millions of dollars from the government of Canada to pay for Native children in provincial schools. The fact that Native people living in urban areas of the provinces pay the same school taxes as anyone else plays no role in decision-making.

Aboriginal Day is another *let us make the air smell better* exercise. Except for in the NWT, Aboriginal Day is not a statutory holiday. Even in FN communities, it is not always a paid holiday, and people get a day's pay docked if they do not show up for work on that day. The latest *let's make everyone feel good but do nothing more* policy is Reconciliation Day.

It Looks Like We Are Doing Something

The fourth reason solutions do not work is the "it looks like we are doing something" solution. Over the years, there have been studies made, at great expense, as well as royal commissions, national inquiries, and other exercises creating volumes and volumes of good work and recommendations for government action with no results. All this work is an end in themselves and were never intended to be used for actual solutions. The people involved in the work, whether they be presenters or the people who compiled them and wrote the recommendations, were dedicated people doing incredible work. There can be no fault found in what they have done. The fault lies in the original objective. The objective is not to develop a plan of action but to give the appearance of developing a plan of action. When it is done, everyone will be happy and will eventually forget about it. Try remembering all the studies and recommendations. The finished report becomes the solution.

Consultation

Another *appearance of doing something* is consulting with Native leaders. Because of the communal fallacy, governments never consult with the people living on the reserves, only the leaders are consulted. Every community leader in Canada knows that consultation means the plan is already written and approved by the policy-makers, and the objective of the consultation is to sell the plan.

The more diverse the leaders consulted, the easier it is to sell the pre-written plan because the law of averages guarantees someone somewhere will say something that is in the plan, and they can say "See, we got it right."

Leaders who take the consultation seriously and come to the sessions prepared with well thought-out recommendations soon discover the plan has already been laid out with little room to move. The rule of thumb in government consultation is the bigger the scope of consultation attempted, the less effective the input. Hosting consultation sessions with large groups is a guarantee that the original plan will come through the session unchanged.

Too Little, Too Late

The fifth reason solutions don't work is the "too little, too late" solution. When it come to the Native people of Canada, epiphany always seems to come too late for well-meaning politicians and their advisors. Former Prime Minister Paul Martin's Kelowna Accord is the best know *too little, too late* solution. The accord may have been a serious attempt to begin the process of finding solutions in many of the areas that are troubling for the Native people of Canada. The resources made available by the accord were adequate, if not to fix everything, but to begin an irreversible march toward a solution. The problem was it was too late in Paul Martin's minority government mandate. The liberals were no longer in the position to carry out the plan. On winning the next election, Harper scrapped the plan.

There is irony in the fact that many of Harper's advisors at the time, and the members of the Harper government near the end of the Harper stretch, came to understand the depth of the problem, finally learning that it was the fault of the system and not the fault of the human beings they only knew as Indians. Their epiphany also came too late.

"Let's Fix Something, Anything."

The last and most agonizing of the reasons that solutions don't work is the "fix something, anything" solution. Responsible government cannot be seen to do nothing about any of the problems under their jurisdiction. It is one of the cornerstones of democracy. It is the very meaning of responsible government. When it comes to Native people, the problems that have accumulated and continue to accumulate have become so diverse, complicated and impossible to be dealt with without a major retooling of the entire system. And the government must still be seen to be doing something. That something is always a highly visible problem like the clean water problem. The government will attack the problem with no regard to the systemic government misguided management that caused the problem in the first place, and they will develop elaborate processes to make it appear as if the problem is being worked on. The *fix something, anything* problem-solving approach is a huge waste of scarce resources and does nothing to improve the lives of the people living on Canada's reserves. If the country of Canada were governed by the same philosophy of fixing one thing at a time, Canada would be in serious trouble within twenty years.

The people who are responsible for creating the policies and programs are all directed by the governments in power. This includes governments in power directing and steering the activities of national and provincial Indian organizations through controlling their funding. It is known by the people on the receiving end as the flavour of the month. Even though the Native people of Canada are the most studied people in North America, they are still the most misunderstood people in Canada. All the planning to develop programs and find solutions never involves the people—their voices are never heard.

There is an endless line of community people who attend national and provincial conferences and stand at microphones to explain and talk about the real needs back home. They talk about the hopeless poverty, the uncaring health care, the substandard education experience for their children and grandchildren, the deplorable living conditions, and most of all, they talk about their frustration with a system that never listens. The best that speakers from the community can hope for is strenuous applause, a pat on the back, and maybe even a group hug. Even though they accomplish nothing with their elegant speeches, they can at least claim bragging rights back home and tell their people "I really told them."

No one listens, not even the leaders they elect and rely on; no one appears to pay attention. They are in fact listening, but they have heard it all before and know they do not have the authority to create change. The system of gathering information for the development of solutions is controlled by the department, and the department's real job is to protect the government in power, not protect the Indians from government. This is the opposite of the role of the Bureau of Indian Affairs in the United States. The Indian leadership, and the federal and provincial organizations are all driven by the flavour of the month.

The Assembly of First Nations' leaders and employees are a hardworking group devoted to improving the lives of the Native people of Canada. Without the AFN, the voices of the people may never be heard. The issues of the people living on Canada's Indian reserves may never be brought to light.

CHAPTER 11:

Major Misconceptions

All democratic governments are in a constant state of review—almost all.

In a democracy, government by the people means progressive improvement. Even when the people make bad choices in choosing their government, democratic procedures have the ability to make corrections. Progressive improvement requires each successive government to build on the successes and learn from the mistakes of the previous government. Building and learning can only be possible if there is orderly transition. Not optional transition rules, but mandatory transition rules and procedures.

Progressive improvement is never guaranteed, and no solution can forever solve anything; there will always be new solutions needed. All democratic governments are in a constant state of review. Making new laws, amending old laws, developing new public policy, changing service delivery systems, and finding different ways to make life better for the governed.

Canada's Indian reserves are still being governed by one archaic law, an outdated public policy, and a delivery system that never changes. For the people living on Canada's reserves, progress is not possible without major changes to the laws of Canada. One of those changes is standard transition rules.

Transition rules are what separates the rule of law from the rule by personal opinion. The rule of law requires that all persons elected to govern must govern by making laws, and they themselves are never above the laws. This means they must obey any and all laws made by any government that preceded them. They cannot simply ignore a law they disagree with.

Band councils under the Indian Act rule by personal opinion because that is how band councils were designed to work. The Canadian public have the mistaken belief that all band councils need to do to improve band government is to change the way they do things within the present system. Band councils cannot change how they do things because they are not governments; they are merely advisors to the Department of Indian Affairs.

The majority of band councils in Canada make a real effort to operate like a government with the well-being of their people as their objective, but a turnover in a band election can and often results in a major turning back to rule by opinion. The Canadian public is still to this day made to believe it is a character flaw in Canada's Native people that prevents good government on Canada's Indian reserves, when in fact everything that happens is either caused or allowed to happen by the laws, regulations and policies of the government of Canada.

New Councillors Are Misinformed

New councillors start out with all of the misconceptions they have heard over the years of being on council. Community members, like all Canadians, have been convinced by the media, consultants, educators, Indian health organizations, Native leaders, government, and all the so-called experts involved in the Indian industry that all that is required to fix what is wrong on reserves is better council members. FN people living in towns and the cities of Canada are even more misinformed, and many believe their people back on the reservation are the architects of their own misfortune.

A fair number of the urban Native population are self-sufficient, have no interest in being involved in community affairs, and prefer not to be bothered by the band office. The information the urban population receives comes from the media, which is always negative, and not only due to the complaints of relatives back home, but also because of the constant negative media statements of overpaid Native leaders. The people living on the reserves, although more aware of the reality of reservation life, are also kept in the dark and have pretty much the same misconceptions as their urban relatives.

New council members, whether from the reservation or the urban environment, all come with the same misconception and misinformation. Reality sets in rather quickly after the staff, consultants and Indian Affairs staff steer them in the preferred direction. They very quickly stop being band members and morph into council members. The preferred direction is always the status quo. It is to the advantage of all above the line of authority to disconnect new councillors from the people who elected them.

There is no advantage for the staff or consultants to fully inform the new council members of the laws or any of their legal responsibilities. The less informed the band council is, the easier it is for the chief councillor, staff and consultants to shape a new council to their liking. It must be remembered that the chief councillor becomes part of the staff after the election, and if the chief and staff are of the same leaning, they can shape the councillors to maintain their advantage. There is a mistaken belief that the council directs the staff. The fact is that the chief councillor is always in control of the staff. It is the chief and staff that create the council agenda and provide the information to the council on which to base their decisions. Councillors are just band members who have moved into an arena with no rules, and they are never told that it is they who have the last say in making and changing rules. Good strong knowledgeable leaders can shape the staff and council to actually make positive change in a community, but again, because of rule by personal opinion, the next leader can reverse community progress and revert to staff and council progress. It does not take long for good leaders to run up against the limits imposed by the Indian Act, and even good leaders will give up and join the comfortable elite above the line between the people and staff.

Newly elected councillors arrive with all the misconceptions they have picked up over the years of being on the outside looking in. They have heard the same misleading information as all Canadians—that the Indian problem is a capacity problem.

Band Support Funding

There is a misconception that chief and council members are paid by the government of Canada, and that Canada provides funding for all the needs of the community. The fact is that bands receive what is called band support funding. This is generally around $250,000 per year and is to be used for operating the band office and basically doing the work of the devolved Indian Agent. It is intended to cover the cost of the administrator and cost of financial accounting and the year-end audit. The remainder of the funds are intended to be used for office costs, such as rent, heat and light, office supplies and all other costs of operating an office. The band administration can be divided into two main functions. The first is to provide administrative function to the band council. The second is to manage the delivery of programs. There are no funds provided by Canada to pay chiefs and councils. Canada provides funding to bands based entirely off funds available in the overall parliamentary budget and never on what is needed or necessary for adequate band government.

In February or March of every year, the band receives a budget package from the department with instruction to sign and return it before the end of March in order to receive funding by early April. The budget package is for education, welfare payments, and other social programs, and is based on funds approved by parliament and the treasury board. There is no consultation, no negotiation and no appeal. Any attempt to argue the amounts stated in the package results in funding being delayed until July or sometime in the fall with no change in the budget package.

Band councils are in the peculiar position of being in control of spending but never in control of revenue. Since the budget package has no link to reality, councils have no choice but to spend where it is needed. It does not take long to acquire the habit of ignoring the budget package and turning their focus to the spending side of management.

The principle of control of spending but not of revenue is the main cause of what the Canadian public views as reckless management. Councils having no control of the revenue process only pay attention to the spending side of management, and eventually, without fail, overspend.

Overspending is inevitable because any spending not in the official budget can be called misuse of federal funds and deducted from next year's funding. All band funding comes from outside sources that require funding applications and are provided to the band at the discretion of the funder. There is no method of internal revenue generation, known as own source revenue, for Canada's reserves.

Own source revenue generally comes from outside the system. Any revenue generated by the reserve's assets, such as timber sales or land leases, must be turned over to the department and held in trust by the department. Any spending of the trust requires the approval of the department. They will only approve community projects; economic development projects do not qualify as community projects by department policy. Government funding to Canada's reserves is for basic survival only, and there is never any intention to improve living conditions on reserves. Canada refers to the policy as the health and safety priority policy.

Health Care Misconception

In Maslow's hierarchy of needs, only the bottom level of the pyramid is allowed by the health and safety policy of the government of Canada. The policy and the misconception about the policy causes no end of problems for the Native people across Canada. The policy is the source of the *Indians get everything for free* myth. The most basic human need is to stay alive, and the policy of providing health care to Native people is designed to do just that and very little else.

The army of professionals delivering health care will argue that prevention is a major component of providing health care, when in fact there is no actual prevention. The prevention policy of Canada consists of workshops and training programs designed in line with the capacity fallacy of laying the blame on the people rather than the system. The fallacy requires fixing the character of the people rather than the policy. Because the policy requires only health and safety needs, no higher actual solutions are ever considered, and if they are, they are always considered to be too costly and impractical. The theory is that to prevent TB, hepatitis and other infectious diseases, workshops are held on the proper way to wash one's hands, rather than building clean water infrastructure.

Windfall Misconception

Then there's the misconception about the windfall. The misconception is on both sides. Many band councils and administrations have been undone by the windfall. The windfall comes in various forms: a specific claims settlement, a benefits agreement with industry, or a consultation and accommodation agreement. Whatever the source, these windfalls are for the most part one-time only or short-lived agreements with no guarantee of continuing. If the windfall was used for much-needed community facilities, such as community halls or recreation areas, or even to pay off financial deficits for housing and public works, or any project that ends when the money runs out, it would be a good thing, but this is rarely the case.

Governments refer to the windfall as "own source revenue." Bands refer to it as "our own money." The term own source revenue is only used by government in reference to Aboriginal governments. Canada and the provinces call it "own source revenue" because even though the revenue has no connection with any normal local government revenue generation process, Canada has made every attempt to make bands pay for services normally provided by the government of Canada and the provinces. The policy of own source revenue is an attempt by Canada to force or coerce band councils to use any money from claims settlements, or payments for loss of use of their traditional lands, to subsidize programs which are federal and provincial obligations.

Windfalls create a cash surplus, not a program surplus. It happens when a large sum of money is dropped into a management control vacuum. There are no rules or standards on how surplus cash is managed; it is fully under the control of the chief and the administration. The federal Financial Management Act, which applies to government, is never enforced on Canada's Indian reserves. Complaints by band members and some council members are never responded to by the department officials. Complaints of band members to the council generally go unanswered or are simply delayed until no one cares anymore.

Because of the nature of windfalls (i.e. sudden, large (in the millions), one-time only cash), it is like a lottery win for the staff and council members. A number of things can happen. For example, if the band had a $2 million deficit and had a windfall of $5 million, it can be assumed the deficit would be taken care of and the remaining $3 million be used for community projects. In some communities, it does happen, but in most communities, this does not happen. What actually happens is the $5 million is spent and the $2 million deficit continues, and in fact begins to grow rapidly.

A large supply of cash suddenly on hand generally means large raises for the chief and management and greatly improved perks for council members. Staff size increases, and more lawyers and consultants become attached to the everyday band operations. And when the money runs out, the higher salaries remain, the council perks continue, the staff size remains unchanged, and the lawyers and consultants have made themselves indispensable. Meanwhile, back on the reservation, the people are still on welfare, housing is still in dire straits, the elders still have to fend for themselves, community facilities remain the same, and ultimately, nothing changes for the people on the reserve.

Over the last fifty years, band councils have been convinced by consultants and lawyers eager for a court case that the government of Canada has a fiduciary obligation to take care of all their needs. While there may be truth in this belief, no court has ever ruled Canada must live up to the constitutional obligation. The result of the belief is that band councils refuse to use any windfall to bump up any government programs—regardless of any shortfall in housing, education, public works, or any of the social programs enjoyed by other Canadians.

It happens because that is an unintended result of the system designed and enforced by the Department of Indian Affairs' bureaucracy. To be fair to the Indian Affairs' bureaucracy, it is the unchanging policies of the government of Canada that is at fault, and it is the bureaucracy's task to carry out and enforce these policies, having no power to look beyond the chiefs and councils.

The health and safety priority policy may sound like a good thing to the people of Canada, but the term really means everything else is not allowed by the department on Canada's Indian reserves. The hidden rule on spending on reserves is the band and the people must not be better off after federal funds are spent than they were before they received it. To most people, this sound ludicrous and unbelievable. The response is usually "that can't possibly be true; no government can possibly have a rule like that." When it comes to Canada's Indian reserves, logic and common sense are not the norm. When the rule is understood, it explains why progress is impossible on reserves.

Health and safety means: if a community has timber, for example, and wants to build a sawmill or manufacturing plant, they will need infrastructure such as roads, water lines, sewer, power and possibly gas lines before a sawmill can be built. The department does not allow infrastructure for economic development because it is not a health and safety problem. Keep in mind, the reserves are owned by the government of Canada, not by the people living on the reserves, so the usual Canadian public argument of *why don't they just borrow the money and do it themselves* is not possible under Canadian law.

The department requires five-year plans from each band, and these plans are used by the department to create the annual budget, required by the treasury board to develop the national budget. The department does not actually use the five-year plans; they are just required to have them. It is only after the national budget has passed parliament that the department officials look at the five-year plans to decide which projects to fund. Most of the approved infrastructure projects are small projects, and expensive projects like new water systems are pushed aside.

Infrastructure for economic development is never considered for two reasons. First, they are not health and safety projects. And second, the creation of assets is not allowed on reserves. Before any development creating assets can take place, Aboriginal title to the land must be surrendered to the government of Canada. Canada has softened the image of surrender by calling it "designation," but the process for surrender and designation is identical. The effect of federal and provincial Indigenous policy is one of Canada's best kept secrets.

Indian Act Misconception

The one major misconception new band councils have is the Indian Act. The most talked about law in Canada is a law that no one has ever read. If the "one law for all" people ever picked it up and read it, their envy of Indian rights would end abruptly. Both the Canadian public and band members, including band councils, have the mistaken belief that the Indian Act protects the rights of Indians. It does just the opposite. The act is designed to limit the basic human rights enjoyed by other Canadians.

Almost all people in Canada believe it is the Indian Act that protects Native hunting and fishing rights. There is no mention of hunting and fishing rights in the act. Food fishing laws and regulations are in the federal Fisheries Act. A little-known fact of the food fish law, Native people do not own the fish they catch. They can eat or store the fish, but not sell, give away or trade the fish. This is because of the communal fallacy, meaning property rights are not considered to exist in communal societies.

An example of the absurd restraints on Indians is the transport of salmon. A sport fisherman owns the fish he catches and can ship his catch anywhere in Canada, but an Indian cannot transport salmon without a permit from the Department of Fisheries and Oceans. University students in the south are able to receive their care packages of canned salmon because airline and bus employees tend to ignore a law they have trouble understanding.

Good Intentions and Next Steps

Good intentions quickly fall by the wayside once reality sets in. With very few exceptions, all who are elected to band councils for the first time start out with the intention of making things better for the people who elected them. They all start with the belief they can make a difference. The fact is they actually have very little power to make any real changes. The only way band councils can make a difference in their home communities is to convince the real powers to make the change. The success of convincing the powers is very limited to the most talented and tenacious band leaders.

Most band councils, no matter how long they are in office, will spend most of their time in meetings out of the community, hoping to convince the powers to make changes. All it takes to have a meeting is for some to agree there will be a meeting. All bureaucracies, whether Indian Affairs or Health Canada, have become adept at giving council members a sense of accomplishment. Meetings usually end with a commitment to next steps. These "next steps" generally mean a date for the next meeting. A major commitment is an agreement to fund hiring consultants to study the problem and make recommendations on more next steps.

The real cycle of life on Canada's reserves is the cycle of next steps, meetings, recommendations and back to next steps, more meeting and so on. Councillors start out believing the meetings are the avenue for change, and it is not long before meetings become the accomplishment.

Councillors have told their constituents that travelling to meetings shows they are working for the people. The people have become so accustomed to it that the response to a question like "I have a meeting with the department next month on that very issue" becomes a satisfactory answer. The meetings and travel have become the status symbol of Indian politics. Chiefs and councillors bask in recognition by airline security workers, hotel doormen and clerks greeting them by their names, and through their recognition by the people in large meeting rooms. The good intentions very quickly become lost in the endless cycle of travel and meetings. Meetings are the core or what has become known as the Indian industry.

The Mandate Misconception

In a functioning democracy, the electorate is presented with choices of various plans of action by the candidates. These plans are communicated through a series of promises. Once elected, the candidate is expected by the electorate to carry out the promised plan. In a functioning democracy, it is understood by both the electorate and the candidate that the elected body has the authority and the ability to keep the promises made during the campaign. It is the promise that elected officials are judged on at the end of their term. It is not only the promise of the candidate, but the overall promise of the political party to which the candidate is attached.

The main cornerstone of a functioning democracy is the promise or plan of the candidate, modified by the promise of the political party. It is always understood by all, except the media, that not all promises can be kept. It is the plan of action that is important, and failure to fulfil the promised plan means failure in the next election.

The dictionary definition of the word mandate is *an authorization to act given to a representative.* In a democracy, it is understood that elected representatives present their plan of action during the election campaign, and winning the election is the authorization given by the people to proceed with the plan of action laid out in the campaign. The mandate is the trust placed in elected representatives by the voters. Elected officials are judged by the voters on whether they carried out all they promised they would. Failing to carry out promises is punished in the next election. Voter punishment also happens if the elected official makes major changes in the mandate without going to the people for a new mandate. The election system works in a democracy because of the mandate rule. Without it, there can be no trust in any of the politicians.

None of this happens in band councils.

Indian reserves under the Indian Act are false democracies—they are democracies in appearance only, not in fact. The key is that band councils are not governments; they do not have anywhere near the powers the people of Canada and the Native people think they have. The powers of the band council are one of the least understood and misrepresented functions in Canada.

This misunderstanding by candidates running for council is one of the major causes of council members failure to carry out the promises they make in band elections. There is no reason to believe that candidates have no intention of keeping the promises they make during the campaign. All have experienced federal and provincial elections and have experienced the campaigns of these elections. They have seen the building of the mandate in other elections; they have read about the how governments are required to operate under a mandate and how they are required to get a new mandate if the plans change. People running for council for the first time have no reason to believe they are also building a mandate during the campaign.

Mistraining

There are no colleges or universities teaching the truth about how bands actually operate.

Training programs sponsored by the Department of Indian Affairs and Indian organizations focus on corporate board management, and much of the training has no resemblance to actual band operations. They are mainly personal capacity building exercises based on the "make better Indians" principle, rather than actual training on the reality of band operations. Practically all training programs involve such things as visioning, mission statements, community planning, land use planning, strength/weakness opportunities, and threats (SWOT) workshops. All of which are corporate board capacity building exercises, and all completely ignore the existence of the people living in the communities. Councillors taking the training come away believing a successful band office is a successful band. All of the government approved consulting firms teach the same courses. And these are all courses designed by people with no experience or knowledge of the reality of the people living in the community.

Attempts to improve training always uses the same resources used to develop earlier misguided training programs for an endless cycle of misguided training. The information to develop these courses are always the existing band council members and the band staff; no one ever asks the community members who are affected. The communal fallacy. Asking the council members and staff for advice on what training is needed will always mean advice on improving conditions for the council members and staff and never to improve the lives of community members. No amount of studies will remedy the problem because the studies always use the same methods, ask the same questions, ask the same group of people, and use the same consultants.

The mandate system of governing that democracy relies on in the rest of Canada can never be made to function on Canada's Indian reserves because for a mandate system to work, the elected officials need the authority to make change. Band councils under the Indian Act only have the authority to manage what is existing, and can only make changes within the existing rules. They cannot make real change.

There are many bands in Canada who have succeeded in making change, but as long as they are governed by the Indian Act, that change will be reversed when the visionary people who made the change are no longer in power. The Indian Act was designed only to allow management of what exists, and leaves powers over progress in the hands of parliamentarians. This makes progress impossible because Native issues in Canada are at the very bottom of parliament's list of issues. The communal fallacy drives the actions of parliamentarians in that they refuse to make new law on Native issues unless all of the bands across Canada agree. While that may sound like an honourable objective, the fact is the Native people are as diverse as any other group of people. And yet it is expected by the government that the people who rely on the government will all think the same.

A rule of thumb on the reservation is a band council is only as good for the community as the staff they hire, and the staff is only as good for the community as the current group of council members. There are bands who have the good fortune of having both good leadership and good staff, and these are the bands who make real community progress. In the end though, the real key is the dedication and honesty of the staff, and their ability to get the work done. Community progress means that the people living on the reserves receive the benefits from council and staff who are doing actual work for the benefit of the people. No amount of good intentions and dedicated work can change the economic or social conditions on Canada's Indian reserves, but by dedicating the meager available resources to improving the lives of people, some progress can be made. Councils working with staff and concentrating on community improvement can channel available resources to make a difference.

When conditions in a community are perpetually bad as they usually are on Canada's reserves, capable and talented people prefer not to run for council and would much rather employ their talents elsewhere. This is a perfectly natural human desire. This is not unique in Native communities, but is the norm in all societies. What is unique in Native communities, because of the communal fallacy perpetuated by the government of Canada, is the criticism heaped on capable people by other Canadians for failing to improve the lives of their people. The majority of Native people across Canada are successful individuals who have become successful by their own ambition and hard work, the same as any other Canadian.

One of the most difficult and annoying effects of the communal fallacy is the criticism and abuse heaped on successful and wealthy Native Canadians by their fellow Canadian citizens, including their fellow Native citizens.

The ludicrous notion that all Indians are the same and get all of their money from the government, and the ones with the most money must have stolen it from their people, is a constant theme in circles where the plight of Native people are discussed. Non-Native Canadians have more myths about Canada's Indigenous population than the Indigenous nations have myths.

It must be remembered that the communal fallacy is not something unique to Indigenous people but is a colonial creation and continues as a policy of the government of Canada and the provinces. It is still Canadian government policy that there are no individual rights on the reserves—all rights are communal. This policy is legislated in the Indian Act. Even modern-day treaties are worded to say all rights are held by the tribe and Canada refuses to include the words saying individual Indians have rights. There is no legal basis for Canada's position, it is just policy. When asked about the policy, the response is always "because that's what Canada wants." They offer no other explanation.

The communal fallacy demands all Indians are supposed to be poor. Although there is truth that a small number of individuals take unfair advantage of their fellow members and the system and enrich themselves, the vast majority of well-to-do Native people make it on their own in the same as any other Canadian. Each time there is a news story of a highly over paid chief, the communal fallacy creates the public assumption that all chiefs are highly over paid. The other fallacy that kicks in is faulty logic, which states: *Indians are poor, and he is an Indian. Therefore, he is poor. If he is not poor, he must taking it from the tax payer.* Good, honest, hardworking people who are well-off because of their own efforts are reluctant to run for band councils because of the criticism from not only Canadians but from their fellow members for not sharing their wealth.

CHAPTER 12:

Cumulative Fallacy

The assumptions and rationalized ideas of the nineteenth century have become today's fallacies and misconceptions.

Much of Canada's Indigenous public policy is based on selective information or false assumptions. Some of these fallacies are fabricated by policy-makers to justify or make palatable unjust objectives. Most fallacies are misunderstandings of the reality of Native people.

Many policies are the result of lobbying by Native organizations on the advice of lawyers and consultants, never from the advice of their band members. The rarest of policy triggers come from recommendations of Royal Commissions, national inquiries or national commissioned studies. It is largely understood by Native people that these commissions and inquiries are ends in themselves, their main purpose being to create the illusion of serious consideration.

There will never be agreement on the elimination of selective information and false assumptions permeating Canada's Native public policy unless they are separated and eliminated one at a time.

The government of Canada continues to view Native peoples as a communal group requiring a single one-size-fits-all. Native leaders, even though they have a wide range of community issues, pet projects and an endless list of grievances, also insist on a one-size-fits-all solution. The combined view of government and Native leaders severely limits involvement from the people living on reserves in any discussion.

Over the past fifty years, I have made every effort to understand the nature of these policies and legislative roadblocks that make progress a futile exercise for the people living on the reserves under the Indian Act. I have spent a lifetime trying to understand and explain the real or root causes of exclusion in a land of abundance. Commonly used labels such as racism, colonialism, prejudice, discrimination, profiling, stereotyping, systemic, and many others are fine for labeling injustice, but none of these terms carry nor suggest any useful action or solution. The challenge is to find and identify the practices creating and maintaining the conditions described by the labels. It is easy to toss around terms like systemic racism and expect the sympathetic ear of governments to leap to our aid. Sympathy has never solved any problem in any real way. The difficulty lies in defining and uprooting the actual culprits causing the mistreatment of Canada's Native people.

The term *cumulative fallacy* is an extension of the term *false attribution*, defined as appealing to an irrelevant, unqualified, unidentified, biased, or fabricated source in support of an argument. Cumulative fallacy is continuing to use the original fabricated source in determining successive action and making no effort to correct the original fabrication.

The beginning of cumulative fallacy goes back to contact and requires an in-depth study that is far beyond the scope of this book. The fallacies affecting Native people were deliberately created by the colonial powers and continued by successive governments under the advice of long indoctrinated bureaucracies. Real and meaningful change cannot be made to happen even with the most sympathetic government. The government of Canada cannot even begin talking about anything resembling reconciliation without the creation of an entirely new bureaucracy, allowing the old baggage burdened team to fade away. Change can not happen using the same machinery which created and perpetuates injustice.

Communal

The first cumulative fallacy that continues to cause no end of problems is the label *communal*. It was originally used in the early 1800s, when the majority of Canada's population were Indigenous people, as a tool to deny registered private land ownership to Indigenous people. The argument at the time was since Indians were communal, they had no concept of private property, so therefore only non-Indians by law could register ownership of private property. The Homestead Act of 1904 in British Columbia, for example, says, "Any person other than an Indian or Chinese may homestead in British Columbia." The communal concept is so deeply ingrained in the machinery of government and industry that all their actions remain skewed by the fabricated communalist argument.

The concept has been around for so long that the Canadian public, governments, and First Nations leaders included, believe it to be true. As an example of the official use of the concept: Indian Commissioner Hayter Reed in 1889 reported to then Superintendent-General Edgar Dewdney of the work begun on remaking the Indian character. The report stated, "The policy of destroying the tribal or communist system is assailed in every possible way and every effort made to implant a spirit of individual responsibility, instead." *Historical Development of the Indian Act* (89)

The false notion that Indians do not have a spirit of individual responsibility persist to this day. The member of parliament for Kenora defines his riding on his twitter page as 56,000 northerners and 42 First Nations. It is standard practice in Canada by all including the news media to refer to non-Natives as individuals and Natives as communal groups.

In Canada, there is an abundance of successful individual Native people—lawyers, judges, doctors, actors, leaders, corporate managers—every profession includes successful individual Native people, even federal and provincial ministers. Even with the highly visible success of individuals, the deeply rooted Canadian view of the communal reservation Indian persists. To be fair, it is not only the Canadian public who hold this view, most Native leaders from local to national hold this same view.

No Native person living on the reserve today has ever known individual freedom. They have grown up convinced that the fabricated communal Indian is the norm. Most believe communalism is the basis of their identity as Native people. It has become a firm belief by all Canadians, including Indigenous leaders, that it is necessary to continue a communalist system inside a democratic country like Canada.

Capacity

The second cumulative fallacy is the label *capacity*. The official policy of early contact was that Indigenous peoples were considered unsophisticated and not as intelligent as Europeans. This official policy applied to all encounters, including in India, Africa, Australia, the Americas, and anywhere colonies were established. The policy was a convenient justification for the tera nullius doctrine. The theory being, Native people never had the capacity to develop a method of land ownership, therefore the land was considered empty by Europeans. This false assumption persists to this day.

A quick search of the Department of Indian Affairs' website revealed the word "capacity" is used 1,740 times. For example, in the department's "Governance Capacity Planning Tool" program application, the following is intended to explain what the "tool" is to be used for:

The Governance Capacity Planning Tool has been aligned with the General Assessment and Readiness Assessment so that any First Nation that wishes to achieve a higher score in the General Assessment or the Readiness Assessment in the future may develop a development plan for core governance which targets the same areas of capacity.

The entire essence of the Canadian (circular) Capacity policy is captured in that one sentence.

Canada's Aboriginal capacity policy creates a never-ending paradox with consultants and Native leaders working to solve a nonexistent capacity problem. The paradox being the more plans created, the further away the solution becomes. The real problem is the existence of the policy itself; the policy creates the problem. Consulting firms love the policy and can crank out no end of proposals and reports that no one reads by simply using the search and replace function to create the same report from community to community. Reports are often only used to check off a box in some other report. Band councils and Native organizations also love the policy because it is an endless source of capacity-building dollars which they and their respective staffs can use to work on solutions to nonexistent problems.

Government buildings and band offices across the country are filled with volumes of unusable reports and recommendations for solutions to a nonexistent problem. Every national or provincial gathering of Native leaders produces new and innovative nonexistent capacity problems needing new funding. Much of the work being done on capacity is on creating documents that seem to show progress is being made with the emphasis on the appearance of progress. The appearance of progress has no effect on the people in the communities, other than having to listen to their leaders' exercise what they view as bragging rights at provincial and national gatherings.

The effect of the capacity policy in education, for example, generally means watering down the curriculum. School boards and school administrators are convinced by the policy conveyed to them by advisors that Native children do not have the same capacity to learn as non-Native students. Band education workers also have been conditioned by the federal policy that they administer that their students must be treated differently and insist on special treatment. Special treatment in practice means lower expectations. Provincial schools have been convinced, even though they do not have the knowledge or expertise, that academic learning should be tempered with cultural teaching. An example of cultural teaching is the course in elementary schools on blueberry picking. The teachers believe they are teaching culture, while in fact they are teaching a skill that can only be used as a berry picker in the berry farms of the Fraser Valley.

The result of the cumulative fallacy of lacking capacity is the perpetuation of the idea and belief in Canada that the collective intelligence of FN people needs to be raised to the level of their neighbours before they can be allowed to progress. The policy can be renamed the 'Make Better Indians' policy and the label would explain the objective of the capacity policy. Schools can not be faulted for perpetuating this view of Native children; the fault lies with the policy, and the Native leaders and band employees who benefit from the policy.

Programs

Every existing or new program, whether created by the government of Canada, the provincial governments or First Nations run organizations, however well intended, starts by building on the ever-growing foundation of cumulative fallacy. Previous programs and policy have long been built on erroneous assumptions and these assumptions continue to be used by policy-makers as guidelines for the development of new policy. These programs, developed and designed at great expense, are recognized by most Native leaders and their administrations as having no benefit to band members, but they see the programs as another source of funding.

In a self-government study carried out by the Northwest Tribal Treaty Group in Northern British Columbia, a retired former regional director, hired to explain how programs are developed, wrote in part:

Departmental policy processes are even more opaque to the public and stakeholders. Policy is formulated through interdepartmental advisory groups and central agencies such as the treasury board with little or no input from those groups or members of the public that may be impacted or affected by the outcome.

With no input in the development of new programs, band administrators see little benefit for the band members and make no pretence at making any effort to improve members' lives. New programs developed by the department are largely designed to alleviate the department's own administrative burdens and have little impact on the people living on Canada's Indian reserves. Administrators who bend the rules and find ways to make use of funds to tackle actual problems are admonished by department officials for misappropriation of federal funds.

To be fair, many department officials are sympathetic and understand the problem and will often turn a blind eye. Sympathetic and understanding officials as a rule have rather short careers in the department.

A huge industry has grown around the task of turning the wheel that serves the few and ignores the many. There is no money to hire FN community members to work on community solutions, but there is no shortage of funds to hire consultants, lawyers, or advisors to tell the people they have a problem.

It is common public knowledge that if there is a crisis in a northern Native community, a plane full of advisors, grief councillors and self-proclaimed professional healers will arrive at great public expense and public fanfare. The main purpose is to create the illusion the problem is being dealt with. When they all leave to write their respective reports, check the appropriate boxes and add to the ever-growing, dust-gathering report archives, the original problem remains unchanged, and may in fact be worse because the money needed by the community to find their own solutions has been consumed by contracted saviours.

The paramount objective of government bureaucracy in these cases is for their political masters to survive the media storm. Once the storm dies down, the problem is considered to be handled. The real objective is always to deal with it—get the problem out of the way and out of the public eye. Even if the word *solution* is used, it in fact means *find a way to deal with it*. No bureaucrat ever wants to inform their superior of any problem in their area; a problem means a disruption in the normally smooth operation of the department. Blaming the messenger is standard bureaucratic practice, and middle managers avoid as much as possible the role of messenger.

Federal government programs are attempts by the government of Canada to duplicate programs and services provided by provincial governments to their citizens. It is not commonly known that Native people on reserves are excluded from using or applying for provincial services. Provincial services, such as education, social services, fire protection, health services, road maintenance, and a host of services taken for granted by the provincial citizens, are denied to people on reserves. The Department of Indian Affairs and Health Canada are the creators and deliverers of these programs, but they lack the know-how and expertise of provincial employees, resulting in substandard programs. Native people are not entitled to any of the privileges in the provinces they live in, nor are they entitled to the privileges offered by federal departments except the Department of Indian Affairs and Health Canada.

CHAPTER 13:

Below the Divide

Before 1969, the line dividing the FN and Canada was Canada and the bureaucracy above the line and Native people of Canada below the line.

We will now examine in some detail some of the reasons people never get heard in the system. Native leaders toe the line for a reason, it is not a character flaw as believed by most of the Canadian public. The people who develop and execute the programs are in the most part acting in good faith and are merely doing what government policy requires. Their only contact with the people being served is through what the system allows, never with the people affected. They only see what is put in front of them. Even if they personally know what they are doing will solve nothing, they are doing the job they are paid to do, and this includes the national, provincial and local Native leaders.

Self-Management

There are many who argue progress is being made, and things are slowly getting better for the Native people of Canada. This argument is only partially true. It is true that the top end of Indian existence, that is the band leaders, band employees, band consultants, band lawyers and the government employees, never had it so good. The Indian industry is good business.

It is not true for the Indians who live on the reserves.

The people in the communities are mere commodities used to fuel the Indian industry. The people responsible never see beyond the band office, and the band office likes to keep it that way to keep their bosses happy. The problems for the people have grown in the past fifty years since the introduction of self-management. The correct term is *self-management* not *self-government* or *self-determination* or any other university paper generated label that make it appear that band councils are in control. The fact is they are not in control; they are simply managing what they are told to manage using tools, rules and policies they are required to use.

A quick look can tell us the true story of Indian existence in Canada. Conditions that did not exist in the 1950s were given birth by misplaced objectives, and not only perpetuated, but also made worse by the principle of compound error. The push for proper housing that began in the 1950s after WWII has not only been a failure, but has created even more problems. The movement to improve utility infrastructure at the cost of billions has, with a few exceptions, made things worse. The clean water problem on reserves is an example. Mercury and other pollutants are on the increase. The list is long, and it is no secret. What is a secret is the system itself. The system that created the problem and the system that perpetuates the problem.

This book examines the system itself and how it affects the self-management of bands across Canada, and the effect on the people that live on Canada's Indian reserves, maintained by one of the wealthiest and resource rich countries on the planet.

A Greater Divide

The interpretation of the intent and function of section 91(24) of the Canadian Constitution resulted in removing Canada's Native people from the Canadian reality. The Native people were set aside and continue to be sidelined by successive governments of Canada. A more accurate description would be to say that the Native people were deliberately, by law, set below the Canadian reality.

The divide between Canada and the Native people is maintained and managed by the Department of Indian and Northern Affairs. The name has been changed several times to attempt to give it a more humane sound, but the purpose is the same—to maintain the divide. From confederation to the Trudeau Government's White Paper policy of 1969, the dividing line was firmly between the Indians and Canada. The line is still firmly in place, but since 1969 has evolved to becoming entrenched on a different plane.

In the Native reality, there are five levels of main players. First is the government of Canada, second the Department of Indian Affairs' bureaucracy, third federal, provincial and local Native service and lobbying organizations, forth the band councils along with their staff, and fifth, at the bottom, are the people living on the reserves.

Before 1969, the line dividing the plane was Canada and the bureaucracy above the Native people of Canada. The 1969 White Paper proposed policy triggered a nation-wide rebirth of Native culture and identity. The Native leaders saw the White Paper as a plan to, by law, exterminate the identity and culture of all Native people of Canada. The White Paper proposal brought to the forefront the great Native leaders across Canada. Up to this point, the Native leaders were mainly engaged in battling for local improvements with the local INAC bureaucracy.

The national battle to defeat the Liberal government's 1969 "Statement of the Government of Canada on Indian Policy" (better known as the White Paper policy) awakened the slumbering rebel in Native leaders across Canada. Native leaders across Canada, following the lead of Cree leader Harold Cardinal, were successful in getting the government of Canada to shelf the White Paper policy. The awakening began the gradual movement of the Native leadership, separating them from the people living on the reserves and urban centres.

The newfound voice was at first successful when used against front line bureaucrats who were accustomed to having the Native leaders and band staff follow their instructions. The beleaguered bureaucracy soon learned the best way to avoid confrontation was to set up buffer organizations to isolate themselves from the abuse of disgruntled Native leaders. The government of Canada began to fund organizations of every description and required Native leaders to deal through the government-funded organizations.

The constitutional patriation debate and the conferences of the 1980s produced no results for the Native people on the reserves, but succeeded in moving the national Native leaders above the plane with bigger fish to fry, leaving their constituents behind. It was the beginning of a greater divide that eventually raised the Native leaders above the dividing line between the people living on the reserves and the band councils.

A side effect of the buffer organizations' program was to accelerate the movement of the Native leaders from below the line, separating the government of Canada from the Native population. The buffer organizations created the illusion that the leaders had some control, and the organizations gradually became the council's constituents. The division between the Native people living on the reserves and the band councils along with the band administration staff gradually moved above the line, leaving the people behind below the line to basically fend for themselves.

The Canadian government's "Government to Government policy" is one of the major contributors to the separation of the band councils and the people. The growing trend toward resource revenue sharing is also contributing to strengthening of the line between the people and power. The appearance that things are improving for the Native population is an illusion. No amount of clamor and complaints by the people below the line has been able to convince anyone that improvement on reserves is an illusion. The real improvement is above the line between the people on the reserves. As the line thickens, the worse off the Native population get. The more power the band councils acquire from financial gain, the less power the people on the reserves have. The thickening line is the result of the accumulation of fallacies, misplaced objectives, legislative vacuum, and the belief by all above the line that they are on the right track.

The people in the communities have received minimal benefits from the changes and what has been called progress. There are of course some exceptions to the preceding statement. As shown above, the separation between the people and the band councils has been growing since the 1960s.

At first, the idea of self-management was heralded as a major step toward self-determination, but events have proven this to be another false assumption. Some band offices are a well-oiled machine, designed to run the office as efficiently as possible and not allow the people in the communities to interfere with the smooth running of the progress above the line. Bands attempting to operate below the line and make a real attempt at improving the living conditions for their community have had some success, but in the end, when the well-meaning people are replaced, the line returns. And with the return of the line, any progress in the community can be reversed in the first month of a new administration.

Government policies and programs, even though well-intentioned, are based on false assumptions, and so they generally result in the opposite of their intended result.

The Social Housing Failure

Social housing is one of the best-known failures. A failure that continues like a runaway train that cannot be stopped, and no one has any idea how to fix it. Social housing is based on rental housing, and bands are required to administer on reserve housing as if it were a business.

The fallacy of "making better Indians" by making people with little or no money pay not only the rent but the maintenance has resulted in the worst housing conditions in Canada, and created bands so far in debt that there is no solution in sight. There is no effort anywhere in the country to find a real solution. Each new idea to correct the problem increases the compound error effect.

It is important to point out that the plight of homeowners has no effect on the operation of the band office. The band councils can simply ignore the problem with no consequence to themselves as councillors. The real problems experienced by the members have no effect on the operation of the council and band staff.

The Conservative government's market housing initiative was an example of a misguided idea that had no hope of getting off the ground. Someone forgot to tell the policy-makers that it was not possible to create market housing on land owned by the government of Canada without creating full ownership for the people who lived in the houses.

Meanwhile, back on the reserve, housing conditions worsened. If someone asked the policy-makers why they continued to dream up ideas that don't work, the answer would have been "That's what we are supposed to do, just doing our job." And they would have been telling the truth.

* * *

The education program based on false premises has resulted a poorly educated Native population. Most high school graduates must spend an additional two years of upgrading just to get into college or trade school. The same is true in the field of economic development programs on reserves. The standing joke in most communities is that we hire an economic development officer at $100,000 a year to tell us there is no money to do anything. Developing an economy on land not owned by the people is not possible. Band members who complain or make suggestions for improvement are always told by their leaders, "Thank you for the suggestion, but our consultants know best."

The department has a favourite experts directory, and these are the consultants used on any of the government-funded projects. The real talent of those on the directory is knowing how to work the system. Bands can choose the consultants but must pick from the list if they want to get funded. Local knowledge is paid lip service and is rarely considered because the consultants can overrule the local people. Not because they have the answers, but because councils and government employees assume consultants know best. Locals are seen by the department officials as advisors to projects but allow the consultants to have the final word. All band administrations know that using the recommended expert means not only approval of a project but more money for administration. The unintended result is less money to go around and fewer projects, and the problem grows faster than the solutions. The list of unintended results below the line is long and growing.

The "Make Better Indians" Fallacy

The most harmful of all fallacies is the "make better Indians" fallacy. This is not intended to be derogatory in any way but an attempt to emphasize the fallacy as clearly as possible. The fallacy is based on the belief that it is the Indian character that is to blame for what is known in government circles as *the Indian problem*. Pointing this out to government officials always results in the stunned, deer in the headlights response.

The fallacy affects all parts of the Native condition. And not only education on reserves, but school districts pay little attention to Native students because of the general belief that *nothing can be done so do not waste time on them, just let them pass and get them out of school.* It is extremely difficult for a Native to get a high paying position anywhere in Canada because of the fallacy. It is a fallacy because Native people are as capable as anyone else, but these very capable people are considered by governments and industry as exceptions rather than the norm.

This is true of Native communities across the country. Band councils would much rather hire non-Native people for key positions and key advisors than hire their own members or members of other bands. Changing the notion of the Indian character flaw is almost impossible because even though Native leaders do not believe they have have a character flaw themselves, they still believe their own members have this flaw.

Capacity Wall

Every new initiative or study runs up against the capacity wall. The word *wall* captures the problem far better than the word *roadblock* since a roadblock requires a conscious effort by someone to stop something. No one is manning the wall; it was simply built more than a century ago and left standing. The faulty logic of circular reasoning is always present in any new initiative. The reasoning of *the Indians are having problems because they are Indians* is built into the criteria of any new initiative or study. The capacity wall has loomed over FN and their employees and consultants for so long that it has become a fact of life. The wall not only looms over FN but over government policy-makers and all government employees, including the ministers and deputy ministers of all departments.

The belief that Indians exist in a different reality from the rest of Canadians is evident. In studies intended to measure the progress of Native communities, all of them are measured against other Native communities, never against neighbouring non-Native communities. Depending on who is conducting the study, all of them are biased in one direction or the other. If the government makes the study, it is usually designed to prove some government initiative or program is working. The government studies are always carried out by people on the approved consultants list and are carried out using the same approved methods. Government studies are generally carried out to justify something or to calm the waters. The results are usually a well-designed layout with recommendations that never get implemented. If recommendations are carried out, they are usually recommendations that have some kind of benefit to the department.

If the studies are done by a FN organization, the results and outcomes depend on who is paying the bill and the expected result. All FN organizations are driven by grant or contribution funding and are completely dependent on the funder. Often the funder is the government of Canada and satisfying the objective of the funder is always the ultimate goal. For the sake of continued funding, FN organizations maintain the illusion of the alternate Indian reality. Since FN organizations have no other possible source of funding, it is an unbreakable cycle. If the applicant does not meet the funding agency's criteria, there is no funding. Therefore, there is no usable outcome from any of the studies, and the only benefit is the appearance of something being done; a few people are employed to conduct the studies and the funding agency managers can say they did their job.

Collective Mental Block

Any attempt by anyone to make a comparison between FN people and the general Canadian population is always, without fail, met with a collective mental block by both the government employees and the band and FN organization leaders. Band members actually believe they are treated in the manner that they are because "that is the way it is supposed to be." The only complaint from the band members is that the band council should do a better job of doing what they are supposed to do. Since they *are* doing what they are supposed to do as required by the government of Canada, the complaints are endless, and the complaints are considered by the councils as simply the price of doing business.

Most councillors just learn to live with it by avoiding the people as much as possible. Travelling to look for solutions is always a good excuse to avoid facing the people. The travel industry in FN meetings continues to be a lucrative industry, and meetings have become a solution in themselves. The common response to the question "What are you doing about it?" is answered by the chief councillor with "I am going to a meeting in Vancouver about that very thing." The complainer feels he/she has accomplished their goal.

Band councils do all they can to defend the system because if they admit they are doing the wrong things, they know they could lose the next election. There is a paradox in the fact that courageous leaders who admit they are doing the wrong things and start doing the right things are the most successful leaders in Canada. Courageous leadership is rare because the collective mental block is insurmountable to the average leader; it takes an exceptional personality to step over the collective mental blockade.

The mental block of government employees is easy to explain. They simply say, "We are following the rules." And they are telling the truth. They are just following the rules.

CHAPTER 14:

The Rules Apply to No One

There is an over abundance of policy, legislation and enforcement to control Indigenous people but a vacuum of policy, legislation and enforcement to free their voices.

In Canadian jurisdictions—cities, municipalities, school boards, regional districts, parliaments, and all governing bodies—training is not required for leadership because the support systems are already in place. Accountability is legislated. There is a body of laws, rules, standards, and procedures that govern and control the conduct of not only newly elected members but all members regardless of experience. All elected people and the employees in the system must obey the rules. Everyone is aware of the penalties for ignoring or circumventing the rules. Everyone is aware that due process will eventually uncover any missteps or misdeeds large or small. If the rules do not work or serve no purpose, there are established open procedures to make new rules that do work.

Bands under the Indian Act have no such rules.

There is no legislated requirement for band council and staff accountability. The band members have no legal method to hold misbehaving council and staff accountable. Band council elections are not the remedy Canadians believe them to be. In a democracy, it is true that elections are the remedy, and new accountable governments make the changes the people electing them have the right to expect. The difference is that in a democracy, elected politicians have the legal authority to carry out the changes they promised. In band elections, the elected politicians have no legal authority to carry out any meaningful change.

In a constitutional democracy like Canada with the accountability requirements of a true democracy, people elected in one level of government can influence the actions of a higher level of government. Band are excluded from accountability requirements. Being outside the system of democratic government, they have no way, other than through public opinion, to influence any level of the Canadian government. Public opinion in Canada rarely if ever works in favour of Canada's Native people. Canadians firmly hold on to the long held false belief that the Native people are the architects of their own misfortunes.

The Accountability Ladder

To examine closely the problem of accountability as it applies on the ground, it is best to start with the people most affected by the lack of accountability. The people living on Canada's Indian reserves are at the extreme bottom end of the accountability ladder. The communal fallacy ignores the fact that reserve communities are made up of more that just band members with band numbers. Like any Canadian community, reserves are made up of band members, members from other bands and non-Native people of all shades; all are first and foremost human beings. The communal fallacy assumes only band members live on these reserves and all are the same and must all be treated the same.

Almost all of the people living on the reserves are at the bottom end of the ladder. The exceptions are the federal employees and contractors who live in the communities. Living conditions for nurses, teachers and other professionals employed by Canada are well taken care of by the government of Canada.

Being at the bottom end means the people possess no powers to affect any of the people above them. Having no effect is not from a lack of trying. People have used direct action protests, like occupying the band office, to no avail. Complaints to INAC officials simply get redirected back to the band office and the chief. The mainstream media usually focus their stories on how *the Natives are restless*. The general public takes little notice, or if they do, it is usually with the *they are at it again* view. Provincial and federal Native organizations, if they become involved at all, will do the same as INAC and will only involve themselves with the councils and staff. They will try to calm the people down with standby responses, such as "Solutions will be found going forward." The bottom of the ladder means the people bear the brunt of Canada's misguided approach to FN accountability.

Using the term "bearing the brunt" is not intended to be an exaggeration. The people on reserves are used by the government of Canada to punish wrongdoing by staff and council. All of the accountability methods use cutting off or threatening to cut off dollars for essential services as punishment. Deliberately reducing Native people to basic survival needs is not new in Canada. It is impossible to continue the fight for your rights or for a piece of the Canadian pie when your children and grandparents are hungry.

Complaints and suggestions by the people living in the communities tend to only make matters worse for the members. Chief councillors and staff often punish what they view as the troublemakers by denying them employment or moving them to the bottom of the list for all services. If the Department of Indian Affairs responds and finds wrongdoing, the punishment is to cut off funds. This results in the people paying and the culprits being free to move on.

When told about this, Canadians generally do not believe it. Those who do believe it write it off as exposing the character flaw in Canada's Native people. Canadians are unaware that under the Indian Act, the Minister of Indian Affairs is the enforcer, the prosecutor, the judge and the executioner all rolled into one. Band councils are a creation of the act and are an extension of the minister and the INAC bureaucracy. Therefore, the minister never takes action against the council; the action is always on the people. The people literally bear the brunt and are helpless to do anything about it.

Communal Punishment

The provinces provide zero services to reserve residents. None of the services available to provincial residents are available inside the reservation boundaries. The provinces provide no health services, no education services (kindergarten, elementary or secondary schools), no social services, no welfare payments, no assistance for the elderly, no road maintenance—in short, nothing. Any services provided by the provinces, such as garbage collection, water, road maintenance, health services, education, etc. must be purchased by the band. Native children attending provincial schools must be paid for by the band through contract agreements.

Everything comes from the government of Canada. Cutting off funding means stopping all of the above services for the reservation residents. In other words, punish everybody. Why? Because they are Indians and Indians are communal. Canada and the provinces do not see Native people as individuals; they only see groups. In the rest of Canada, it is the individual person committing the unlawful act who receives the punishment. On the reservation, the wrongdoers can simply move on to something else and the people are arbitrarily punished.

An example of the use of communal punishment is the Accountability Act passed by the Harper Conservatives. It is important to remember, the Department of Indian Affairs' bureaucracy are the advisors and drafters of this piece of legislation. The Accountability Act requires band councils to list the band audit report and post on the department's website all monies paid to council members. The punishment for failing to post the report is cutting off all of the federal funding, thus punishing the people, not the council, not the staff, and not the auditor.

The act was a failure as a method to hold elected people accountable because it served no purpose other than satisfying Harper's Conservative base. It did not make any band council any more accountable than they were before the act was passed. Accountability to the people living on the reserves was not included in the act, but it was the people who were punished for the failure of their band councils. The communal fallacy makes it inconceivable for the Department of Indian Affairs' bureaucracy to view council members as individual wrongdoers. They are seen a part of the whole, and any wrongdoing by any part of the whole means punishment for all. Contrast that with any small town in Canada where any illegal act by a city council member is an individual act, and the individual is charged, not the entire town.

The Ones with the Hammer

Accountability is nonexistent on Canada's Indian reserves because there is no legislative foundation for council and staff accountability. The only rules are those included in the financial transfer contracts between the department and the band councils. The only way to accurately describe the arrangement is to say, "The culprits are responsible for enforcing their own accountability." There is no external enforcement mechanism. The rules that are made by band councils are never followed because it is left to the councils themselves to enforce the rules, and there is no penalty for failing to enforce the rules.

It is human nature for whoever drafting the rules to make the rules favour themselves and the people approving the rules. Even well thought-out rules never work because an incoming council will either ignore the rules or simply change them to more council-friendly rules. The system in practice places the band councils and their staff above the rules. So, in reality, the rules apply to no one. A complaint by a member is usually met with the answer, "We have rules in place to handle it." And that is the end of the matter.

Native leaders from chief councillors to National leaders argue that all they need is the authority and jurisdiction to make the laws necessary for accountability, and the problem will be solved. The argument, however noble, will not solve the accountability problem because the council and staff will still be above the law. The reason they are above the law is there is no external vigilance or enforcement. Even if the council passes a law requiring the council members and staff to be accountable to the people, they can ignore it whenever the requirement becomes inconvenient. If there is no external monitoring and enforcement, it is the staff and council who, by default, end up with the monitoring and enforcement powers.

People holding the hammer will never hit themselves on the head. Rule of law can only exist if there is independent external enforcement; the independent magistrate is a democratic cornerstone. There is a belief by Canadians that Indians on reserves are exempt from the laws of Canada and the provinces—this is simply not true. In most cases, the reserves are simply excluded when it comes to enforcement; provincial and federal prosecutors do not like to get involved in what are known as *Indian issues.*

Another problem with the hammer is that the ones with the hammer will hit their enemies but not their friends. We must be clear that this phenomenon is not peculiar to Native people; it is simply a natural human trait. The western United States became the Wild West because the hammers were held by individuals. Favouritism, nepotism, patronage, partisanship, and all human failings are common to all human beings on the planet. The difference is that in a democratic society, there are laws and conventions to control human urges when people become part of government. And on Indian reserves, the Indian Act makes no mention of fairness to the people. The hammer welded by the councils is a hammer of exclusion. People on reserves who are considered by council members or staff to be troublemakers, or enemies of the chief councillor, are excluded from homeownership, post-secondary education, home repairs and any other service. All of this is legal under the Indian Act. It is legal because the act is silent.

How to Dismantle the Line

The actual on-the-ground problem of accountability includes financial accountability, political accountability, mandate accountability, ethical accountability, conflict of interest and transparency. In practice, the current accountability path is upward to the Department of Indian Affairs. The problem requiring a solution is the line dividing the people living on the reserves and the people governing them. Until that line is dismantled, there is no workable answer for the people. The question is how to dismantle the line.

The first obstacle to dismantling the line is the government to government (G2G) policy. Band councils are not governments, even though they can, and increasingly do, create the illusion that they are governments. It can be argued, and is most often argued, that band councils are a form of government, but they are most certainly not democratic governments. A more accurate definition is: band councils are boards established by the Indian Act, acting on behalf of the Minister of the Department of Indian Affairs. Due to their limited powers to make meaningful change, band councils rarely discuss long-term issues in council meetings. Practically all issues on council agenda are immediate issues. By maintaining the position of only dealing with band councils, the government of Canada provides them with an easy method of avoiding any interaction with the people.

The real interaction between the councils and Canada is between the chief councillor and the funding officer. The Department of Indian Affairs is a typical government bureaucracy in that it operates top down. The funding officer's powers are limited and can only operate within the scope of their job description. Instructions and policy come from the top, and lower level employees like funding officers have no authority to make any changes. They can only make the minor adjustments within their limited authority. Like the old time Indian Agents, their powers are over the band councils; they have no powers to affect anything above them in the department chain. Band councils regularly meet with various department directors and middle managers, but the problem is the same at any level of the department. Department employees can only deal with matters within their allotted cylinder.

A majority of chief councillors, provincial and national Native leaders insist on G2G because it is the one policy that gives them enormous power over not only the people but over all band business, operation, and policy. First Nations with self-government agreements or modern day treaties and who have also installed constitutional democracy through a public constitutional development process with their members, do not have this problem because they are democratic governments—in fact and practice.

In a constitutional democracy, the voice of the people can not be ignored for very long. Indian Act bands have no such controls. Even though band councils can develop elaborate rules for council members' conduct, council accountability, conflict of interest, ethics, etc. these rules can simply be ignored or changed at the council's whim. The reason councils can make changes on a whim is because the entire Indian Act system is based on individual council members' personal opinions and not on any rule of law.

Self-governing First Nations, on the other hand, operate under the rule of law through their constitutions. The reason G2G is an obstacle is that the majority of elected chiefs prefer the status quo since it maintains their personal independent power. Unlike self-governing First Nations, the people's voices never reach the ears of the policy-makers, and the majority of Native leaders at a national conference will always vote against any measure that will curb their personal independent power.

A major mistake made by the government of Canada is to use national political organizations as the sounding board for national Indian policy decisions. National organizations are so far removed from the people on the reserves that they actually become entities unto themselves, and their organizational interests become paramount to the people's interests. The separation is not by design. All national organizations start out with the intent of improving the lives of the people on the reserves and in urban Canada. All national organizations have good, hardworking, dedicated leaders with good intentions. No matter how hardworking and dedicated the leaders are, the organizations are eventually overtaken by the need for self-preservation, and that need for self-preservation eventually becomes the paramount objective.

It can be argued that it is the individual chiefs who control the national assembly, and this is in fact true, but the diversity of the Native people of Canada makes it impossible to be of one mind on any issue. National organizations are particularly good at tackling specific objectives, such as the residential school matter, but the diversity of First Nations across Canada make it impossible to tackle overall national policy issues. Canadian citizens think having ten diverse provinces and territories with two official languages is a problem. The diversity of the First Nations people are at least ten fold that, but the government of Canada continues to attempt to address Native issues with the belief that Indians are all the same and must all be entitled to the same solution. Canada attempting to get national agreement on major policy matters, such as education, using national organizations will always fail because of the natural national diversity.

To overcome the G2G obstacle, the government of Canada must first find a way to connect with the actual people living on the reserves and urban centres of Canada. Opening the door to the people means first recognizing them as individual Canadians as diverse as any other Canadian. The fifteenth century policy of communalism can only be changed by law. The communal policy has been intrenched in the Canadian experience for so long that it is believed by the Canadian public, including Native leaders and by every person in government elected or employed. That it is the way Indians must be viewed "because they are Indians."

Recognition as individual Canadians does not mean a repeat of the 1969 White Paper policy. The vast majority of the Native people of Canada have an unshakable desire to maintain their identity as Native people. Native people consider themselves different from other Canadians in the same way French Canadians consider themselves different. They also, like French Canadians, want to maintain their culture, languages, and unique way of life. One of the great fallacies of Canadian public policy is the long-held belief of all Canadians that the Indian Act is the only vehicle capable of ensuring the difference. Aside from the official Languages Act of 1969, the French do quite well in maintaining their culture without a French-Canadian Act. Culture and language is natural and does not need laws and policy to thrive. It does, however, need to have the laws and policies designed to suppress it from being removed. Any bureaucrat, government representative or Native organization who says, "We are already doing that" does not understand the problem. The biggest and almost insurmountable obstacle is getting the powers that be to admit they have been wandering down the wrong road, and are still wandering down that same wrong road.

Consultation with national organizations, provincial organizations and band chiefs on a strategic approach will only result in repeating history. All will use familiar practice of hiring lawyers and consultants and other professionals to prepare their positions and responses.

Lawyers, consultants, and other professionals, by the nature of their business, will always produce results favourable to the group signing their cheques. This is not a condemnation of professionals, only a statement of fact—pleasing their clients is how professionals make their living. The history being repeated by the above approach is deliberately staying above the broad line dividing the Native leadership from the people. All of the work and planning will be done above the line with no input by the people below the line. The result will be more power for the chief and organizations and no change for the people living on the reserves and in urban centres.

To reach and understand the people below the line requires strong political will by the government of Canada. A process that does not start with the people will result in a win for the Native leaders and a loss for the people living on the reserves and in Canada's urban centres.

The Trudeau Government move, Justin that is, of dividing the department in two is a possible good first step, provided that a new and different bureaucracy is created as well. If both departments use the same bureaucracy, use current department officials as advisors or transfer managers from the old to the new, little will change. It is the experience of FN in the use of consultants that former government employees turned consultants carry departmental baggage with them and continue the departmental culture and long-established norms to which they are accustomed. The use of former government employees as consultants by band councils works today because they understand and know how to work the existing system and are highly effective in what they do. The same is true of FN organizations.

Organizations will use the same lawyers and consultants, using the same methods, under the same instructions to use the same research material and so on. Designing and building a new on-the-ground system that works for the people is a entirely different ball game. The existing system has not only created the current dysfunctional system, but has perpetuated it for so long that it has become the accepted norm in Canada and that includes the FN leaders and organizations.

FN organizations local, provincial or federal, all face the same constraints on their ability to recommend any real change. They all serve two masters, neither of which is the people. Their first and most powerful master is the government of Canada. Canada's power over First Nations people of Canada is arbitrary, meaning they can do whatever they want, whenever they want, and the people have no method available to them to do anything about it.

It is arbitrary not because it is required, but because that is how section 91(24) of the British North America Act turned Canadian Constitution is interpreted by governments since confederation. Governments and the bureaucracy prefer to use the section as meaning they have authority over Indians and lands reserved for Indians. For the government of Canada to change the view to interpret the section as a *responsibility* rather than an authority will take enormous political will on the part of the prime minister, whoever the prime minister may be.

The government of Canada's real power is stopping or limiting the activity of bands and organizations. No one can force anyone to do anything they don't want to do, but it is possible to remove or make all other options undesirable or impossible. Using their arbitrary power, departmental bureaucrats cut off or deny funding to bands and organizations if they stray from the government's planned course.

Bands and organizations have made attempts to make better use of available funds with innovative ideas and have been stopped by the department with the line "You are free to carry out the program in any way you choose, but since it no longer fits the funding criteria, we are no longer able to fund the program." The only way bands have been able to get around the arbitrary power is to not tell department officials their plans and manufacture acceptable progress reports.

Canada adheres to and applies the communal fallacy across the country. What works in a community in northern Ontario is expected to work on the BC West Coast even if there is no problem on the West Coast. Why? Because Indians are communal and must be all the same and managed the same. The result is bands who have no need for the program apply for it anyway because it means more program dollars for the band, even if the program serves no purpose.

CHAPTER 15:

Individual Indigenous Rights

The Native people of Canada do not need sympathy or comforting words, they need action.

Changes needed in Canada must be done and not simply discussed, studied, and pondered. Any serious work done in Canada by Royal Commissions, national or provincial inquiries or studies all end with a list of recommendations. Recommendations that never turn into action—real change requires action. The 2017 and 2019 activity surrounding reconciliation is centred on changing the relationship between the government of Canada, the provinces, Indian organizations, and band councils, with no apparent plans or even any suggestion to change the relationship with individuals on Canada's Indian reserves.

The current push to reconcile makes no effort to include the people living on the reserves and in the urban areas of Canada.

Our leaders will argue that it is about the people, and provide lists of their members to show as proof. It must be remembered, in the firmly established system which has been allowed to evolve over the last one hundred years, the constituents of the organizations and the band councils are not the people who elected them. In practice, these constituents are the department, the organizations, the lawyers and consultants, and increasingly, the private industry. Band members are not lists and numbers, they are human beings—they are the forgotten people of Canada.

Band members are forgotten by the federal government, the provincial governments, national and provincial Native leaders, and worst of all, the majority of band councils. FN service organizations have taken over the "I know what is best for you" role of the Department of Indian Affairs. Unless the problem of freeing the band member from the two-hundred-year-old shackles of individual obscurity is addressed systematically, deliberately, and unilaterally by the government of Canada and the provincial governments, all of the efforts in the reconciliation push will end up on the dusty shelf.

Every Native person in Canada, who is not part of a band council or is a leader or part of a leadership of in an organization supported by band councils, has a voice that no one hears, a voice no one is obligated to listen to, a voice no one wants to hear. The statement will no doubt break the record in "that's not true" statements pouring from chief councillors, consultants, lawyers, and government employees. It is entirely contrary to the interest of the leaders and governors to free the voice of the people.

The consultation process in place today has never worked for the Native individual. The process was designed to serve the legal consultation requirements of government, where predetermined plans are presented to leaders to fulfill the government's legal necessities. More importantly, the process serves the chiefs and councils well because they can control the input and ensure an outcome advantageous to maintaining their power over the members. It must always be remembered that it is not the intention of the chiefs and councils to ignore the people, nor hold power over them, but this is the unintended result of cumulative Indian policy over successive Canadian governments.

It must be emphasized that maintaining power over the members is not a character flaw and must not be overlooked or passed off as a "because they are Indians" argument. All of the laws of Canada, except the Indian Act, reflect and enforce the principles of a democratic society. Section 91(24) of the Canadian Constitution has been interpreted, since the enactment of the British North America Act, to mean laws governing Native peoples of Canada must be governed by different laws. These are the laws that have successfully excluded Native people living on Canada's Indian reserves from the benefits of being Canadian. The interpretations may have been the intent at the time it was written, but there is nothing in the constitution requiring that interpretation to continue indefinitely.

At the time of the writing of the British North America Act, the so-called *Indian problem* remained unresolved. Section 91(24) of the BNA Act took what England considered the unresolved Indian problem and transferred it to the federal government of Canada through the clause. Subsequent governments to the present day cling to the false assumption that the Indian problem must remain unresolved. The resource industry relies on the continuation of this assumption. Native leaders have been convinced that to maintain our identity as Native Canadians, the Native people must not only live under different laws, but also must remain under a fiduciary "wards of the state" relationship to avoid endangering the policy of communal culture. As stated earlier, communal culture is not the natural state but is a convenient policy to maintain the status quo.

The communal policy, one of the original false assumptions, which created the problem to begin with, actually prevents even looking for solutions. Communal policy prevents the government of Canada from conducting direct community discussion groups made up of band members and the people who live with band members on the reserves. The policy requires the approval of the band council and band office to conduct community discussion groups. And experience has shown, if band councils see a threat to their power, they can and have withdrawn their approval. Staff have the ability to stack the meeting by not only handpicking participants, but they can also control the information presented to community members. Staff also freely use the practice of labeling any resident a troublemaker for speaking out. Under the Indian Act and the communal policy, this is all perfectly legal. Legal in the sense that there is no law that prohibits it.

Government's response to criticism is the circular argument that it is what the people want, and when asked how they know this, the answer is *the leadership told us*. Government policy requires federal and provincials governments to only deal with the people through the chiefs and councils and never directly with the people. The communal policy is a brick wall that no one has the courage to breach or to even acknowledge that it exists.

The failure of Canada and the provinces to recognize Native people as individuals with individual rights creates a barrier to accurate and truthful information on the real condition of Canada's Native population. Chief councillors and leaders of Native organizations prefer to keep it that way, in the same way that they fought for exemption in the Canadian Human Rights Act with the claim that it infringes on their communal rights, when in fact it denies even the most basic individual civil and human rights to their members.

The most troublesome concept in the Indian Act is the arbitrary power the chief and council are granted in the act. The act effectively denies all the band members any due process guaranteed to other Canadians by the Canadian Constitution, in any decision and in any part of their lives on reserves. The Indian Act gives the chief and council the power to make life-altering decisions based purely on whim, and the minister holds the authority to give legal force to the decision based on whim. The minister and his/her minions exercise that authority simply by doing nothing. Due process, a component of the principles of fundamental justice in Clause 7 of the Charter of Rights and Freedoms, is eliminated for individual band members by the existence of the Indian Act.

In practice, the legal authority to act on a whim means chief councillors and the band administrator owe no accountability to the band members. They can do whatever they feel like doing, no reason is required, and they will be supported by the

Minister of Indian Affairs. Band members questioning the chief or staff usually get the response "because that is our decision" or "it is council policy." There is no legal requirement to provide any further explanation. The history of government inaction is demonstrated by a statement made by a community elder I was sitting beside to a Minister of Indian and Northern Affairs who was visiting his community in coastal British Columbia. He said, "The next time you want to meet with us, just send us your picture and we will put it on a chair and talk to it."

An example of arbitrary power in the Indian Act is Clause 20(1) *No Indian is lawfully in possession of land in a reserve unless, with the approval of the minister, possession of the land has been allotted to him by the council of the band.* In practice, the clause does two things. First, it gives the chief and council the power to discriminate. And second, it removes any property rights from any individual band member.

For example, an applicant for land can and is often rejected because the applicant is a member of a family on the chief's enemies list. If there are multiple applicants, family and friends of council members top the list. Even in a bidding process established by the council, the chief's family can somehow acquire insider information about the perfect amount to bid. The words *possession of the land has been allotted* has no qualifiers. There are no procedural rules, no right of appeal, no accountability process, no checks and balances. In short, the individual band member has zero property rights. Lawyers who defend the council's action will say the member can always go to civil court. They will say this while being fully aware that no band member in Canada has the financial resources to go to court, nor a chance of winning because the government of

Canada will defend the council's action since a court loss means the Indian Act will likely require amendment.

There are many successfully run bands in Canada. These are bands with leaders who understand the system and how to work it. These are bands who ignore the established rules, and create their own rules aimed at providing for their people. Lessons can be learned from these leaders; they have a clear understanding of the necessary steps for real reconciliation to happen. The simple secret to their success is they pay full attention to the individuals who elected them, putting the needs of their constituents above the needs of the band and the staff. The continuing problem is that if the leaders are replaced, the system self-corrects.

The first necessary step in reconciliation is an act of parliament removing, by law, the communal notion and legally recognizing all Native Canadians under section 91(24) of the Canadian Constitution as individuals with individual rights, including individual Indigenous rights. It would require a new law which includes amending the offending sections of the Indian Act. To do this would take enormous political will on the part of the government of Canada because all levels of Native leadership will view the move as a limit on their power over their respective members. The need for such a law IS to limit the powers of current band leaders and organization leaders over their members. Self-determination by the people must be the goal, not self-determination by the leadership and band staff. A more accurate statement is, the purpose is to move the power from the band council members to the people. The dividing line between the members and the chief and council is deeply entrenched, and if the government of Canada requires the approval of the Assembly of First Nations chiefs, the people living on Canada's Indian reserves will remain completely powerless.

To paraphrase a Churchill quote, a people powerless to make change can be very easily kept powerless because the people who do have the power will never voluntarily relinquish it to the people.

Changing the long-held policy of communalism is a task where strong political will is needed the most. Political will must come from the government of Canada because the problem of diversity among the Native people of Canada makes it impossible for a national organization to develop and maintain any political will. In a national assembly, political unity only lasts until the meeting is adjourned. Real G2G is only workable if the people have the power, real power, to question or effectively petition their governments. That power must be in place before the implementation of real G2G. If it is not in place, the Native people of Canada will forever be subservient to their own elected leaders.

Successive governments have always viewed Native people's concerns as an after thought. Native issues are looked at seriously only when there is nothing important to do, and usually so late in the mandate that the issues end up being shoveled on to the pile of political promises for the next election. For change to actually happen, it must be done early in the mandate while the governing party still has an excess of political capital.

The list of legally sanctioned injustices endured by the people living in the reserves of Canada is long. Every department in the government in Canada and the provinces have laws and policies limiting the civil and basic human rights of Native people.

It has been three hundred and nineteen years since the signing of the first treaty. The Treaty of Albany, otherwise known as the "Great Peace," was signed in Montreal in 1701. Three hundred and nineteen years later, the conflict continues. We are now in the twenty-first century.

Maybe it is time to fix it. Just maybe.

Manufactured by Amazon.ca
Acheson, AB